AF603955

THE GRAND PALACE OF LUCIFER

The Psychology of Dark Minds

Dr.Robin K Mathew

Writer's Pocket

First published by Writer's Pocket in 2024

email:editor@writerspocket.com

Cover Design by Dr. Robin K Mathew

ISBN-13: 978-93-6083-850-8

www.writerspocket.com

DEDICATION

To those who see clearly through the fog of history,

This book is dedicated to the truth that no war was ever waged in the name of the Devil. The greatest horrors of mankind have always been in the name of gods, religions, and ideals that claim divine favor. Bloodshed has been justified with the banners of faith, power, and righteousness, not with the darkness we so often associate with evil.

May we never forget that it is not the devils we create, but the gods we follow blindly, that lead us into the deepest depths of human cruelty. To the innocent children of West Asia, whose laughter has been silenced by the horrors of war,

This book is for you—the young souls caught in the crossfire of violence waged in the name of power, ideology, and faith. As the world watches, your lives are torn apart, not by your choices, but by the cruel hands of those who claim righteousness.

In a hypothetical "state of nature" without government, humans, driven by self-interest, would naturally conflict with one another, creating a chaotic "war of all against all," which is why a strong central authority is necessary to establish order and peace by enforcing laws and maintaining social stability; essentially, individuals must surrender some freedoms to a sovereign power in exchange for protection from this constant state of conflict.

Leviathan - Thomas Hobbes's

CONTENTS

PREFACE

As I stand on the threshold of introducing The Grand Palace of Lucifer: The Psychology of Dark Minds, I am reminded that the human mind is as vast as it is dangerous. This book is an exploration into the darkest chambers of that palace—into the minds of those who use deception, manipulation, and violence to further their agendas, both consciously and unconsciously. Throughout history, we have seen the acts of serial killers, con artists, mass manipulators, and glorified leaders responsible for mass killings—figures often shrouded in myth, fear, and misunderstanding. But beneath these sensationalized personas lies a core of human psychology that is both disturbing and fascinating.

My journey into this subject has been driven by one central question: What makes a mind dark? What drives an individual to deceive, manipulate, and kill without remorse? The Grand Palace of Lucifer takes the reader through various rooms of this metaphorical palace, where we will meet professional killers whose detachment from morality is chilling, and explore the psychology behind lynch mobs driven by collective hysteria. We will confront the charming faces of con artists who exploit human vulnerability, and dissect the methods of religious extortionists who prey on faith to amass power.

This book is not just about serial killers or those whose names have become synonymous with evil. It's about the many facets of manipulation and how they exist in everyday life. In some ways, the tactics used by a political leader inciting violence are no different from those used by a con artist swindling their victim—the difference is only in scale and impact.

Our modern understanding of "evil" is often simplified by narratives that focus on isolated incidents or individual pathology. Through The Grand Palace of Lucifer, I seek to challenge those misconceptions, unraveling the complex web of psychological, social, and historical forces that shape these dark minds. It's a grim subject, yes, but one that is crucial if we are to understand the mechanics of manipulation and exploitation that, in their various forms, continue to shape our world.

As you walk through these pages, you will enter the minds of those who operate in shadows, whose actions have shaped history in blood and deception. My hope is that by understanding these dark forces, we can better recognize them in our own lives—and guard ourselves against their insidious influence.

Welcome to the Grand Palace of Lucifer. The tour begins now.

Robin K Mathew

Part I

The Devil's Workshop

Dark Minds

The Story of Ted Kaczynski

Ted Kaczynski was born on May 22, 1942, and grew up to be a brilliant mathematician. A true prodigy, he had an incredible mind and achieved academic success at a young age. But despite his promising future, Ted's life took a dark and unexpected turn. In 1969, he suddenly abandoned his academic career and chose to live a reclusive life, far away from society. This decision would set him on a path that would make him infamous as the "Unabomber," one of the most notorious domestic terrorists in American history.

Ted Kaczynski's shift to isolation began in 1971 when he moved to a tiny cabin in the wilderness near Lincoln, Montana. The cabin had no electricity or running water. Ted wanted to live a simple life, learning survival skills, becoming completely self-sufficient. But as time went on, he grew frustrated. The wilderness he loved was being destroyed by the growing industrial world. New developments, roads, and machines were taking over nature, and Ted felt powerless to stop it.

This growing anger turned into something more dangerous. Ted became convinced that modern technology was destroying not only nature but also human freedom. He believed that industrialization was controlling people's lives and ruining the natural world. In his mind, the only way to fight back was through violence.

Between 1978 and 1995, Ted Kaczynski launched a nationwide mail bombing campaign. He sent carefully crafted bombs to people he believed were promoting technology and harming the environment. His targets included university professors, airline executives, and others involved in advancing modern science and technology. Over the years, his bombs killed three people and injured 23 others. For nearly two decades, authorities were unable to figure out who was behind the attacks.

The FBI launched what would become the longest and most expensive investigation in its history to catch the mysterious bomber. Since they didn't know his identity, they referred to him by the case name "UNABOM," which stood for "University and Airline Bomber." This is how the media gave him the name "Unabomber."

In 1995, after years of terrorizing the country, Ted decided to make a bold move. He sent a letter to The New York Times, promising to stop his bombings if they or The Washington Post published his manifesto—a 35,000-word essay titled Industrial Society and Its Future. In this manifesto, Ted explained why he believed modern technology was destroying human freedom and dignity. He argued that his violent acts were necessary to wake people up to this growing threat.

The FBI and U.S. Attorney General Janet Reno agreed to have the manifesto published, hoping it might lead to a break in the case. In September 1995, The Washington Post printed Ted's essay, and millions of people read his ideas. Among those readers was Ted's own brother, David Kaczynski. As he went through the manifesto, David noticed the writing style sounded familiar—too familiar. He remembered letters Ted had sent him in the past that expressed similar ideas.

Although it was a painful decision, David went to the FBI with his suspicions. He shared his concerns that his brother might be the Unabomber. With this crucial tip, the FBI was finally able to track down Ted Kaczynski at his remote cabin in Montana. In April 1996, they arrested him and found bomb-making materials, journals, and detailed plans for more attacks. After his arrest, Ted was determined to avoid being labeled as insane. He rejected the idea of using an insanity plea to escape the death penalty, even though his court-appointed lawyers wanted him to. Instead, Ted chose to plead guilty to all charges in 1998. He was sentenced to multiple life terms in prison without the possibility of parole.

In the years following his conviction, Ted lived out his life in prison. In 2021, he was diagnosed with cancer and stopped treatment in early 2023. On June 10, 2023, Ted Kaczynski took his own life in prison, bringing an end to the story of a man who went from being a brilliant mathematician to a dangerous terrorist driven by his hatred of modern society.

The Psychology of Darkness

In the early 2000s, a new area of psychology started gaining attention—Dark Psychology. As the internet grew and crimes moved online, psychologists and criminologists became interested in understanding the minds of cybercriminals, serial offenders, and others who engage in harmful behavior. Their goal was to uncover the darker side of human nature and figure out why people commit such terrible acts. This study became an important tool in fighting crime.

One of the biggest breakthroughs from this work was criminal profiling. This method helped law enforcement understand the behavior of criminals and predict their next move. The famous example of "Unabomber" Ted Kaczynski, was something that evoked the curiosity of the criminologists. With Psychological profiling it helped as a powerful tool for catching dangerous criminals.

Dark Psychology didn't just help catch criminals—it also led to new laws. As more people became victims of online predators, the legal system had to adapt. Previously, there weren't many laws to protect people from cybercrimes or online harassment. Governments around the world responded by creating new laws to help protect individuals from these digital threats.

Instead of only looking at the crime itself, experts began studying the criminals' minds. This psychological profiling helped courts better understand the motivations behind their actions. As a result, many of these offenders received longer sentences and were required to undergo psychological treatment.

Dark Psychology has shown us how complex—and sometimes frightening—the human mind can be. By studying this darker side, we have made significant progress in keeping society safer and better understanding the impulses that drive people to commit harmful acts.

Part II

The Dark Hall of Deception

Traits of Dark Psychology

Let's dive into the key traits of Dark Psychology

I. Narcissism The "Me-First" Mentality

Narcissism refers to excessive self-love, an inflated sense of one's importance, and a lack of empathy for others. The term originates from the Greek myth of Narcissus, a handsome youth who fell in love with his own reflection in a pool of water, ultimately leading to his death. This myth symbolized self-obsession and vanity.

Example -In a romantic relationship, narcissism manifests when one partner consistently prioritizes their own needs, desires, and emotions, often at the expense of the other person.

Here's an example

Imagine a couple, Sarah and John. John frequently makes decisions without considering Sarah's feelings or input. He insists on choosing where they go for dinner, what they watch on TV, or how they spend weekends, always prioritizing his own preferences. When Sarah tries to express her needs, John dismisses them, often making her feel guilty for wanting something different.

Whenever there's an argument, John never admits fault. If something goes wrong, he blames Sarah, saying she's too emotional or sensitive. When things are going well, John takes full credit, claiming he's the reason for their happiness. In public, he seeks constant praise from friends and family, while belittling Sarah's contributions. Over time, Sarah feels undervalued, emotionally drained, and stuck in a relationship where her needs are consistently ignored.

This kind of "me-first" attitude can lead to an unhealthy dynamic, where one partner feels emotionally suffocated and the relationship becomes unbalanced.

In an office there could be a manager who constantly takes credit for successes but blames their team when things go wrong. They crave attention and praise, and this "me-first" attitude can create a toxic working environment, making everyone around them feeling undervalued.

II. Overly Sensitive Egos The Approval Seekers

People with this trait are often known as approval seekers. They constantly look for validation from others and are extremely sensitive to criticism. Their self-worth is based on the opinions of others, so they might make poor decisions just to gain approval.

Example - In a romantic relationship, someone who constantly seeks approval may become too dependent on their partner for feeling good about themselves, which can create problems.

Imagine a couple, Tina and Jimmy. Tina always looks to Jimmy for reassurance. She often asks if she looks nice, if she's doing well at work, or if he loves her enough. Even small disagreements or gentle criticism from Jimmy can hurt her feelings, making her defensive or overly apologetic. If Mark mentions he likes a certain hobby or style, Tina will go out of her way to adopt it, even if it's not something she enjoys, just to make him happy.

When it's time to make decisions, like where to eat or what to do, Tina rarely speaks up about what she wants. She might agree to go to a restaurant she dislikes just because Jimmy likes it, avoiding any chance of upsetting him. Over time, Tina starts to lose touch with who she really is, as she's always focused on pleasing Jimmy. This puts pressure on Jimmy to always reassure her and can make the relationship feel one-sided, where Tina feels anxious without constant praise and Mark feels burdened by having to give it.

This can make both of them unhappy—Tina feels insecure and needy, while Jimmy might feel overwhelmed trying to keep up with her need for approval.

Both narcissism and overly sensitive egos can have dangerous consequences, whether it's someone manipulating others to fuel their ego, like Anna Sorokin, or a powerful leader making terrible decisions to protect their image, like Richard Nixon. These traits are central to Dark Psychology and show how dangerous self-centered behavior can become.

III. Personal Entitlement The "I Deserve It" Attitude

People with a strong sense of entitlement believe the world owes them something. Whether it's wealth, respect, or love, they feel they deserve special treatment just because of who they are. When they don't get that treatment, they often react with anger and frustration. Think of a wealthy celebrity who demands VIP treatment everywhere they go, causing problems when they don't get what they want. That's personal entitlement in action.

IV. The Puppet Masters

Manipulative individuals are like puppet masters, pulling strings behind the scenes to get what they want. They don't care about the ethical consequences as long as they achieve their goals. A modern example might be a political strategist who spreads false information about opponents to win an

V. Moral Disengagement - The Rule Breakers

Moral disengagement happens when people convince themselves that unethical actions are acceptable. They justify breaking the rules without feeling guilt or shame, seeing themselves as above societal norms. This is common in corporate scandals where executives commit fraud, believing that their actions benefit the company, even if it harms others.

VI. Psychopathy - The Empathy Void

Psychopathy is a condition where a person completely lacks empathy. People with this trait can harm others without feeling any guilt or remorse. They are often associated with violent crimes, like those committed by notorious serial killers such as Jeffrey Dahmer, who was able to carry out horrific acts while feeling emotionally detached from his victims.

VII. The Willingness to Harm

Spitefulness is when someone deliberately tries to harm others, often out of anger or frustration. Malice takes this a step further—it's when someone enjoys causing harm, even if it hurts them in the process. An example of spitefulness might be an employee sabotaging a project at work, even though it could cost them their own job.

Part III

The Den of Predators

The Human Predators

Imagine someone who knows exactly how to push people's buttons, using charm and manipulation to get whatever they want. This is a *human predator*—a person who preys on others for personal gain, without feeling bad about the harm they cause. They can show up in all walks of life, from personal relationships to the workplace. These predators exploit others to benefit themselves, often without showing any remorse.

But not all predators are the same. Understanding the different types can help you spot them before they cause harm. Let's break down the most common types of human predators and how to recognize them.

Types of Human Predators

Human predators can come in many forms, including social, sexual, cyber, or emotional predators. No matter the type, they tend to share similar behaviors that reveal their true nature.

a) Charm and Charisma

Social predators often use charm as their weapon of choice. They seem incredibly friendly, confident, and engaging, which makes them appear trustworthy and likable. But don't be fooled by their charm—it's often just a mask.

If someone's friendliness feels too good to be true, or if they suddenly turn manipulative when things don't go their way, you might be dealing with a predator.

b) Manipulation

Manipulation is one of the key tactics predators use. They twist facts, create false stories, and use guilt to control others. Their goal is to get what they want, even if it means lying or playing people against each other.

Watch for anyone who consistently bends the truth or makes others feel guilty to get their way. They might seem like they're helping, but their manipulation is all about serving their own interests.

c) Lack of Empathy

A true predator has little to no empathy. They don't care about the feelings or suffering of others, and in some cases, they may even enjoy causing harm. This lack of empathy allows them to hurt others without feeling any guilt.

If someone seems unaffected by another person's pain or even finds amusement in it, that's a clear warning sign.

d) Pathological Lying

Pathological lying is when someone lies a lot, even when there is no clear reason for the lies. Pathological liars can't seem to stop themselves from lying, even when the lies cause problems in their life. The lies may start small but can become very elaborate and detailed over time. Pathological liars often lie about things that are easy to verify, which can make their lies obvious to others. Some signs that someone may be a pathological liar include

- Telling many lies each day, for longer than 6 months
- The lies don't seem to serve any purpose or benefit the person
- The lies become more and more complicated over time
- The person shows distress, problems in their life, or puts themselves/others in danger because of the lying

If you notice these signs in someone, it may be a sign they are a pathological liar. The best thing to do is encourage them to seek help from a mental health professional, as pathological lying can be a symptom of an underlying condition.

e) Superficial Relationships

Human predators often only maintain shallow relationships, using people for what they can get from them rather than forming real emotional connections. Their relationships are transactional—once someone no longer serves a purpose, they are quickly discarded.

If someone's friendships or partnerships seem more about personal gain than genuine connection, this is a major red flag.

f) Aggressiveness and Intimidation

When charm and manipulation don't work, predators can switch gears to aggression and intimidation. If they are denied what they want, they may resort to bullying, anger, or threats to maintain control.

Notice if someone turns to aggression whenever they face resistance. Predators often use this tactic to scare people into submission.

g) Sense of Entitlement

Many predators believe they are entitled to special treatment. They feel they deserve admiration, success, or privileges—even if they haven't earned them. They expect more from others than they are willing to give in return and often act like the rules don't apply to them.

Be wary of people who consistently expect to be treated better than everyone else, without contributing much in return.

h) Inability to Accept Responsibility

Predators rarely take responsibility for their actions. Instead, they blame others or external circumstances for their mistakes or failures. They're quick to point fingers and avoid any accountability for their own wrongdoings.

If someone is always shifting blame and never owning up to their part in a problem, they might be a social predator.

i) Inconsistent Behavior

One of the most telling signs of a human predator is their inconsistent behavior. They may act sweet and agreeable one moment, only to turn cold and calculating the next. This shift often depends on who they are with or what they want to achieve.

Watch for dramatic changes in someone's behavior, especially if their attitude changes based on how much power or advantage they can gain in a situation.

j) The Chameleon Effect

Imagine walking into a room filled with people. Among them, you notice someone who seems to change like a chameleon. One moment, they're warm and friendly, charming everyone around them with a bright smile. The next moment, their demeanor shifts, becoming cold and calculating, as if a switch has been flipped.

This is the behavior of social predators—people who adapt their actions based on who they're with or what they want to achieve. They can be sweet and agreeable one minute, but then turn icy and manipulative the next. It's as if they're playing a game, and you're not quite sure of the rules.

Keep your eyes open for these sudden changes. When they seem to align with how much power or control the person feels in a situation, it's a red flag. For example, if they are speaking to someone who holds authority, they might act submissive and pleasant. But if they're dealing with someone perceived as weaker, their tone might shift to something more aggressive or dismissive.

Understanding these signs is crucial. By recognizing these

patterns, you can protect yourself and others from falling prey to their games. Trust your instincts—if something feels off, pay attention. Setting clear boundaries is essential when you notice this kind of behavior.

So, the next time you encounter someone who seems to change like the wind, remember it's not just you. Spotting these inconsistencies can help you navigate the tricky waters of social interactions and keep yourself safe from those who thrive on manipulation.

k) The Blame Shifter

One final hallmark of the human predator is their inability to accept responsibility. Mistakes? Those are always someone else's fault. Consequences? Never their problem. They'll twist any situation to make sure the blame never lands on them. If someone constantly dodges accountability and points the finger at others, they're likely hiding their true nature behind a wall of excuses.

Human predators can be masterful in hiding their true intentions, making it hard to see them for what they are—until it's too late. But by staying aware of these signs and trusting your instincts, you can learn to recognize the dangers before they strike. Sometimes, the best defense is knowing what to look for.

Protecting Yourself from Predators

Recognizing these signs is crucial for protecting yourself and others from human predators. They are skilled at hiding their true intentions, but if you pay close attention to these behaviors, you can avoid falling victim to their manipulation. Trust your instincts, set clear boundaries, and don't be afraid to walk away if you notice any of these warning signs.

Part IV

The Devils' Laundry

Brainwashing

Imagine someone slowly losing control over their own thoughts, beliefs, and identity, until they no longer know who they are. This is the terrifying process of *brainwashing*, where a person's mind is manipulated and reshaped to serve someone else's goals. Brainwashing isn't just about forcing someone to do something—it's about completely changing the way they think and feel. To understand how this works, let's explore its origins and the different layers involved.

The Origins of Brainwashing

The term "brainwashing" first gained attention during the Korean War in the 1950s. American prisoners of war (POWs) were subjected to intense psychological manipulation by Korean and Chinese soldiers. These soldiers used brainwashing techniques to erase the prisoners' sense of self, forcing them to betray their country and even confess to crimes they didn't commit. This deeply disturbing method of control sparked fear worldwide and made people wonder how can someone's mind be so completely taken over?

Since then, brainwashing has become a subject of fascination. Whether people want to understand it, use it for their own purposes, or protect themselves from it, brainwashing remains a powerful tool of psychological manipulation that still affects criminal justice today.

The Layers of Brainwashing

Brainwashing is not just one simple trick—it's a step-by-step process designed to break down a person's identity and replace it with a new one. Here's how brainwashing typically unfolds, with real-life examples to show each stage in action

a) Rewriting the Past

The first step in brainwashing is making the victim question their own memories and beliefs. Imagine being told that everything you've ever known or believed is wrong. Over time, this makes you doubt your entire past. A famous example is Patty Hearst, who was kidnapped by the Symbionese Liberation Army in 1974. After being manipulated for months, Hearst began to question her old life and eventually joined her captors in their criminal activities. By making her doubt her past, her kidnappers were able to reshape her thinking.

b) Inspiring Guilt

Guilt is a powerful tool. In brainwashing, manipulators use guilt to break down a person's self-worth. In cults, for example, leaders often make people feel ashamed of their past actions, convincing them that they need to change everything about themselves to find redemption. This guilt makes them more willing to follow the cult's beliefs and seek approval from the manipulator, driving them to abandon their old lives in search of a fresh start.

c) The "All Is Lost" Moment

This is the point where the victim feels utterly hopeless. In abusive relationships, for example, the abuser chips away at the victim's self-esteem until they believe they have no value, no future, and no escape. The victim becomes so broken that they'll do anything to find relief from their despair. At this stage, the manipulator gains even more control over them because they're desperate for any kind of support or solution.

d) Reaching Out with an Offer

Once the person is isolated and broken, the manipulator extends a lifeline—a small kindness or gesture. This act of "compassion" makes the victim feel grateful to their abuser, creating a bond. For example, a prisoner who has been tortured may feel grateful to their captor for a moment of kindness, such as being given food or comfort. This can make the victim see the captor as a potential ally, opening the door for deeper manipulation.

e) Confession and Compulsion to Get Involved

At this stage, the person is so desperate for relief that they start to accept the manipulator's beliefs and actions, even if it goes against their morals. They may confess to things they never did or agree to harmful behaviors just to escape the psychological torment. A real-life example of this can be seen in false confessions during high-pressure interrogations, where innocent people admit to crimes they didn't commit simply to make the torture or questioning stop.

f) Acceptance and Rebirth

In the final stage, the person fully accepts the new identity they've been given. Their old self has been erased, and they now completely believe in the manipulator's worldview. This process is often seen in people who have been deeply indoctrinated, like members of cults or extremist groups, who turn against their own families and former lives to embrace a new, manipulated identity.

g) Reverse Psychology

While brainwashing involves breaking someone down, *reverse psychology* is a more subtle form of manipulation. Instead of directly forcing someone to do something, reverse psychology tricks them into doing the opposite of what you say by pretending to support a different outcome. For example, if you tell a child, "You probably won't like these vegetables—they're for grown-ups," the child might feel challenged and decide to eat them just to prove you wrong. It's a clever way to influence behavior without making the person feel like they're being controlled.

The Hidden Power of Manipulation

Throughout history, in the darkest corners of personal relationships and political movements, certain people have wielded an almost hypnotic control over others. These individuals knew how to bend minds, twist realities, and create worlds where only their voice mattered. The scariest part? Most victims didn't realize they were being manipulated until it was too late.

Let's dive into two gripping examples—one from a tragic historical event, the other from the all-too-common scenario of an abusive relationship. Both reveal the chilling power of brainwashing.

The People's Temple

In the early 1970s, a charismatic man named Jim Jones rose to power, leading what appeared to be a hopeful and inclusive religious group called the People's Temple. What started as a beacon of equality and faith soon became something far darker. Jones, with his intense charm and ability to promise salvation, slowly drew his followers into his web of control.

Jones used a powerful technique—isolation. He pulled his followers away from their families, away from anyone who might offer a different perspective. He moved them to an isolated compound in the dense jungles of Guyana, far from the reach of society. There, in Jonestown, his word became law. Cut off from the outside world, Jones fed his followers a single narrative he was their savior, the one true path to salvation. His message was relentless, driven home through daily indoctrination and sermons. The more they listened, the more they believed.

As months passed, doubt faded, and loyalty deepened. For the followers, Jim Jones wasn't just a leader—he was the only truth that mattered. This intense psychological manipulation reached a horrifying climax in 1978, when Jones convinced over 900 of his followers to drink poison in a mass suicide-murder, known as the Jonestown Massacre. They trusted him, even as he led them to their deaths.

The People's Temple is a terrifying reminder of how isolation and indoctrination can be used to break down individual thought, replacing it with blind loyalty and, ultimately, complete control.

Gasligting

Now, not all brainwashing takes place on such a massive scale. Some of the most devastating forms happen quietly, behind closed doors, where no one else is watching. This is the reality for many trapped in abusive relationships.

One of the most insidious tools an abuser uses is gaslighting. This technique is all about undermining a victim's sense of reality. Imagine this every time you bring up a concern, your partner tells you you're overreacting. They tell you that you're too sensitive, that what you remember didn't actually happen the way you think it did. Little by little, they make you question your memory, your feelings, and, eventually, your sanity.

It starts small. Maybe they deny saying something hurtful, or they twist your words until you feel like you're the one in the wrong. Over time, the gaslighting escalates. You begin to doubt your own thoughts, constantly turning to your partner for validation, unsure of what's real and what's not. This dependency is exactly what the abuser wants—because as long as you rely on them to define your reality, they hold all the power.

In abusive relationships, gaslighting isn't just a form of manipulation; it's a slow, cruel erosion of the victim's self-worth and independence. The abuser rewrites the narrative, always casting themselves as the rational, calm one while painting the victim as irrational or even unstable. It's a mental prison, and many victims feel trapped, unsure of where to turn or how to escape.

Whether it's the tragic case of Jonestown or the more personal horror of gaslighting, these examples show that brainwashing comes in many forms. It doesn't always look like mind control in the movies—it's often subtle, creeping up slowly until the victim feels powerless. But understanding these techniques is the first step in recognizing them and, hopefully, breaking free.

The Devil's Digital Handle

In the age of endless scrolling, where every swipe reveals a new post, video, or ad, most of us have no idea how much control we've given up. Social media platforms like Facebook, Instagram, and WhatsApp are more than just tools to connect with friends—they're finely-tuned machines designed to shape what we think, how we feel, and even how we behave. The most unsettling part? It's happening without us even realizing it.

In many cases, the issues at hand are real, but they are amplified or distorted to such an extent that they provoke extreme emotional responses. This manipulation keeps people hooked—constantly reacting, sharing, and arguing, rather than thinking critically or finding solutions.

Outrage Porn

Outrage porn is the deliberate use of exaggerated or

sensationalized content designed to provoke anger, indignation, or moral outrage. Just like actual pornography manipulates physical desires, outrage porn targets our emotional triggers, pushing us to feel morally superior or righteously angry. Whether it's through news articles, social media posts, or heated arguments, the goal is to keep us engaged by keeping us outraged.

Imagine waking up, scrolling through your social media feed, and immediately being bombarded with posts, headlines, and comments that make your blood boil. Everywhere you look, people seem furious—at the government, at celebrities, at each other. It's like the world has become one giant argument, and you're caught right in the middle.

This flood of anger and outrage, often blown out of proportion, is part of a manipulation tactic called outrage porn. The goal of outrage porn isn't to inform, but to provoke strong emotional reactions, feeding off our desire for righteousness and moral superiority. And it's not just something we see in the news or online—outrage porn plays a big role in personal relationships, politics, and religion, where it is used to stir division, control conversations, and rally people around a cause, whether real or exaggerated.

Let's explore what outrage porn is, why it's so addictive, and how it shows up in different areas of life, often without us even realizing it.

Politics

Outrage porn is rampant in politics. In today's polarized world, political debates are often less about understanding and solving issues, and more about stirring anger against "the other side." Politicians and media outlets exploit outrage porn to rally supporters, keep them engaged, and distract from deeper, more nuanced discussions.

Ex: The Angry Political Rhetoric

Picture a political rally where a candidate shouts to the crowd, "The other party is trying to destroy our country! They're taking away your jobs, your freedoms, and your future!" The crowd erupts in anger, feeling justified in their rage. But here's the problem: while the candidate may be touching on real concerns, the language is exaggerated and designed to inflame. Instead of talking about complex issues like the economy or healthcare with nuance, the speech paints the other party as evil, fanning the flames of outrage.

The more angry the crowd gets, the more they rally around the candidate, feeling like they're fighting against a terrible enemy. This kind of emotional manipulation turns political discourse into a battle of outrage rather than a space for thoughtful debate. The candidate doesn't need to provide solutions because they've already hooked their audience with the most powerful tool of all—anger.

Outrage porn in politics thrives on simplifying complex issues, turning every disagreement into a moral war where one side is righteous and the other is corrupt. It's an easy way to gain support, but it leaves little room for real understanding or progress.

Outrage Porn in Religion

In religious contexts, outrage porn can be used to create a sense of moral superiority, where people are encouraged to feel angry about the behavior or beliefs of others. Religious leaders or groups may use exaggerated claims about the moral decay of society or the persecution of their faith to rally followers around a cause, often leading to division and intolerance.

Imagine a religious leader giving a sermon where they declare,

"We are under attack! Our faith is being threatened by outsiders who want to destroy everything we believe our culture and traditions. We must fight back against this evil before it's too late!" The congregation, stirred by this fiery speech, leaves the service feeling not just concerned, but deeply angry at those perceived to be the enemy.

The leader's language paints the situation in extreme terms, turning a complicated issue into a black-and-white battle. The congregation is left feeling outraged and morally superior, convinced that they must defend their beliefs at all costs.

Here, outrage porn stirs division between different groups, making it difficult for anyone to engage in respectful dialogue or find common ground. The constant state of moral outrage keeps people defensive, making them more susceptible to manipulation and less likely to question the narrative they're being fed.

Why is Outrage Porn So Effective?

Outrage is a powerful emotion—it's immediate, consuming, and often feels justified. When we're outraged, we feel like we're on the right side of a moral battle. This emotional rush can be addictive, especially when it's reinforced by others who share our anger.

It feels righteous: Outrage allows us to feel morally superior, like we're fighting for justice. This makes it easy to ignore any doubts or counterarguments.

It simplifies complex issues: Outrage porn reduces difficult problems into simple, emotionally charged battles between good and evil. It removes the need for deeper thinking or understanding.

It creates a sense of belonging: When we share our outrage with others, it fosters a sense of community and solidarity. This is especially powerful in politics and religion, where group identity plays a big role.

It distracts from real issues: By focusing on exaggerated or manufactured outrage, we avoid having to deal with the more complicated, less emotionally satisfying aspects of life. It keeps us locked in reaction mode rather than solution mode.

By learning to recognize and resist outrage porn, we can take control of our emotions and focus on real solutions to the problems we face. Instead of letting manufactured outrage manipulate us, we can seek out thoughtful, balanced conversations that lead to understanding, empathy, and progress. After all, real change comes not from constant anger, but from meaningful action.

The AI Manipulation

a) Algorithmic Puppetry

Imagine this every time you open your social media app, you're stepping into a carefully crafted world. What you see isn't random; it's the result of sophisticated algorithms that decide which posts, videos, and ads will keep you hooked the longest. These algorithms learn what you like—what you click on, what you react to—and then feed you more of it.

But here's the catch they don't just show you what you like. They filter out everything else. Over time, this creates something called an "echo chamber." It's like living in a bubble where all the content reinforces your existing beliefs and opinions. Opposing ideas are pushed out of sight, making it harder to see the full picture.

This is how polarized thinking starts. Without realizing it, you begin to believe that everyone thinks the same way you do, because that's all you're seeing. Critical thinking fades, and you get a distorted sense of reality, where everything fits neatly into your worldview. It's like being the star of your own show, with the platform quietly pulling the strings.

b) The Power of Emotional Triggers

Have you ever noticed that certain posts just make your heart race? Maybe it's a shocking headline, a story that makes you angry, or a post that stirs up fear. That's not by accident. Social media platforms thrive on engagement, and they know that the best way to grab your attention is through strong emotions.

So, they feed you content that stokes the fire—sensational headlines, clickbait, and emotionally charged stories designed to provoke outrage, fear, or anger. The more emotional you feel, the more likely you are to react, comment, or share. And that's exactly what these platforms want. Engagement is their currency.

Over time, this constant stream of emotional content can warp your sense of reality. Issues that aren't as urgent as they seem are blown out of proportion. And before you know it, you're caught in a cycle of high-intensity reactions, unable to see the quieter, more balanced side of the story. It's all about keeping you hooked, even if it means skewing your perception of the world.

c) The Herd Mentality

We all want to fit in. It's human nature. And social media taps into this desire in a powerful way. Every like, share, and comment you see is a signal—this is what people are talking about, this is what matters. It's called social proof. The more attention a post gets, the more valuable or true it seems.

So, when you see that a post has thousands of likes or shares, it's hard not to be influenced. You start to think, "If so many people believe this, maybe I should too." This is how false information or harmful trends can spread so easily. You're not just seeing content; you're seeing content validated by your peers, and that makes it feel trustworthy, even if it's not.

It's like being in a room full of people all nodding their heads in agreement. After a while, you find yourself nodding along too, whether or not you really agree. That's the subtle pressure of social media—pushing you to align with the crowd, shaping your opinions without you even realizing it.

d) The Tailored Trap

But perhaps the most personal—and unsettling—form of manipulation on social media is found in the ads. Every click, every like, every interaction is tracked and analyzed to build a profile of who you are, what you want, and even what you fear. With this data, platforms like Facebook and Instagram deliver advertisements so perfectly tailored to you that they seem to read your mind.

These ads don't just sell products; they tap into your deepest vulnerabilities. Feeling insecure about your appearance? Here's an ad for a new beauty product. Worried about your future? Here's a financial service promising peace of mind. It is a targeted manipulation, aimed at steering your thoughts and decisions in ways you wouldn't have chosen on your own.

The danger lies in how easily these ads can shape not just your buying habits, but your beliefs and desires. Over time, they can influence your politics, your lifestyle, and even your identity—all while you think you're simply browsing your feed.

e) The Fear of Missing Out (FOMO)

Picture this you're sitting at home, mindlessly scrolling through your feed, even though you have no real reason to. Why? Because deep down, you're afraid you might miss something—

an update from a friend, the latest trending video, or a message that makes you feel included. This is the power of FOMO, or the fear of missing out.

Social media platforms are built to fuel this fear. Features like infinite scrolling, notifications that ping constantly, and the short-lived nature of "stories" all create a sense of urgency. You're made to feel like if you don't check in right now, you'll be left behind. The result? People stay glued to their screens, searching for meaning in content that often lacks substance.

Over time, this behavior can turn into an addiction. You might find yourself more invested in virtual interactions than in real-life experiences. Instead of enjoying the present moment, you're lost in the digital world, looking for validation in likes, comments, and updates. And while you're trapped in that cycle, the content you're consuming quietly shapes how you think.

f) The Lies We Believe

Now, imagine scrolling through your feed and coming across a shocking headline. It's dramatic, grabs your attention, and makes you feel something—maybe anger, fear, or disbelief. Without thinking, you hit "share," passing it along to your friends. But here's the problem that headline might not be true. Social media is a breeding ground for misinformation (false information spread by accident) and disinformation (deliberately false information spread to deceive).

Because posts go viral so quickly, false stories can spread faster than the truth. And unlike traditional media, where facts are checked before publication, social media thrives on speed, not accuracy.

Emotional stories get more engagement, so they're more likely to pop up in your feed. The more shocking or sensational the content, the faster it spreads, and soon, millions of people might be believing in—and acting on—something that isn't true. This can have dangerous consequences, influencing everything from personal decisions to global events.

g) The Ads Know You Better

Social media knows a lot about you—more than you probably realize. Every click, like, and interaction is tracked and analyzed, building a detailed picture of who you are. Your personality, preferences, fears, and desires are all mapped out in data. This is called psychological profiling.

Platforms use this information to predict what you'll do next, and then they influence that behavior with targeted ads and content. Think about the last time you saw an ad that felt strangely relevant to your mood or situation. That's not a coincidence. Advertisers use your data to serve up content that speaks directly to your emotions, often steering you towards decisions you might not have made on your own.

During political campaigns, this profiling becomes even more dangerous. Platforms can target specific groups with tailored messages, subtly swaying opinions and voting behavior. It's like being quietly nudged in a certain direction, all without you realizing someone is guiding your choices. In this way, social media can undermine democracy, shaping elections and public opinion for the benefit of powerful agendas.

h) Normalization of Extreme Views

In the real world, extreme ideas often stay on the fringe. But on social media, they can spread like wildfire. Algorithms that prioritize engagement often push radical or sensational content to the top of your feed because it sparks strong reactions. The more you see it, the more normal it starts to feel.

This normalization of extreme views can make dangerous ideas seem acceptable, even when they're far outside the boundaries of what's ethical or reasonable. When people are exposed to extreme content regularly, they can become desensitized to it, and what once seemed outrageous starts to feel like just another viewpoint.

This process can lead to radicalization. Individuals who might never have encountered certain extreme views in their everyday lives suddenly find themselves drawn into echo chambers, where their opinions are reinforced and pushed further. As more people fall into these traps, society becomes more polarized, with divisions growing deeper.

Part V

The Devil's Tools

Manipulation Techniques

Con artists and manipulators thrive by making the first step seem harmless, the next one inevitable. Their techniques work because it preys on our need to stay consistent with our past actions. The next time someone asks for a small favor, a tiny commitment, or just a quick "yes," ask yourself what's the next step? Where could this lead? Because sometimes, it's not just about the little request—it's about setting you up for something much bigger.

1. The Foot-in-the-Door Technique

This method is all about making someone comfortable with a small, seemingly harmless request, which then opens the door to much bigger, riskier demands. Why does it work? Because once people commit to something small, they feel an inner pressure to stay consistent with their previous actions. This psychological trick can be used in everything from advertising to the most dangerous of scams.

Ex: The Free Trial Trap

You see this trick everywhere today, especially with online subscription services like streaming platforms or apps. They lure you in with a free trial—no money, no commitment. All you have to do is sign up. Easy, right? But once the trial is over, they automatically switch you to a paid subscription unless you actively cancel. By the time the trial ends, you're used to the service, maybe even dependent on it. That small, "free" commitment suddenly becomes a paid one, and many people don't bother to cancel. That's how a harmless little trial snowballs into a monthly bill.

2. The Door-in-the-Face Technique

Have you ever been asked for something so big, so outrageous, that your first reaction was an immediate "No way!" But then, when a much smaller request followed, you suddenly felt like saying yes? That's no coincidence. It's a psychological trick called the Door-in-the-Face Technique, and it works by first overwhelming you with an unrealistic request so that the second, smaller one seems much more reasonable in comparison.

It plays on two key psychological principles contrast (the second request looks much smaller when compared to the first) and reciprocity (people often feel like they should "meet in the middle" after refusing the first request). Let's dive into how this clever tactic works and look at a few real-world examples.

Ex Charity Donation Request

Let's say a charity is raising money for a new community center. To get donations, they use the Door-in-the-Face Technique.

Step 1: The Large Request Volunteers ask potential donors for a hefty contribution, saying, "Would you be willing to donate $500 to help build our new community center?" For most people, $500 is too much, so they politely refuse.

Step 2: The Smaller Request Next, the volunteers say, "We understand $500 is a lot. Could you donate $50 instead? Every bit helps, and we'd really appreciate your support."

Outcome: Now, compared to the first request, $50 doesn't seem so bad. Many people who felt uncomfortable giving $500 are relieved to offer the smaller amount and agree to donate.

The smaller request looks manageable, and most people still want to help in some way, so they say yes.

Ex: Customer Service Negotiations

Here's how the Door-in-the-Face Technique might show up when you're haggling with a cable company for a better deal.

Step 1: The Large Request: A customer service rep offers an expensive premium package "We've got a great premium package for $150 a month with all the movie channels, sports packages, and high-speed internet." Most customers, expecting a better deal, find this price far too high and say no.

Step 2: The Smaller Request: The rep then says, "I understand $150 is a lot. How about our standard package for $80 a month? It still includes high-speed internet and a good selection of channels."

Outcome: After hearing the steep $150 offer, $80 suddenly sounds much more reasonable. The customer feels like they're getting a good deal in comparison to the first offer and is much more likely to accept.

Why It Works?

The Door-in-the-Face Technique succeeds because the first request sets the stage for the second. Once we reject something too big, the smaller follow-up request looks more appealing, even if we wouldn't have agreed to it initially. It's a psychological trick that taps into our need to be fair and reasonable, especially after saying no.

So, next time someone hits you with a big ask and then offers a smaller, more "reasonable" request, think twice. You might just be walking through the door they wanted you to open all along.

3. Lowballing

We've all been there—you see an offer that seems too good to pass up. A new car at an unbeatable price, a cheap flight to a vacation hotspot, or a home improvement project that fits right into your budget. But just when you're ready to commit, the real costs start creeping in. Welcome to the world of lowballing, a sneaky tactic where sellers lure you in with an attractive offer, only to reveal hidden fees and extra costs once you've already taken the bait.

Let's take a look at how this works in everyday life—and even in history.

Ex: The Car Sales Trap

Car dealerships are notorious for using lowballing to reel in customers. They'll advertise a shiny new car at a price that seems too good to be true, and it usually is. Here's how it plays out

Step 1: The Sweet Deal: A dealership advertises a car for $20,000. You walk in thinking you've found a great bargain. The price feels just right, and you're excited to drive off with your new ride.

Step 2: The Hidden Costs: But as the paperwork gets started, extra charges suddenly appear. There's a $1,500 delivery fee, $800 for paperwork, and a $2,000 "mandatory" warranty. By the time everything is added up, the car that was supposed to cost $20,000 is now $24,300.

Outcome: You feel trapped. You've already committed mentally to buying the car, so paying the extra fees feels like the only option. That's exactly what lowballing relies on—getting you hooked before revealing the real cost.

Ex: The Airline Ticket Illusion

It's not just car dealers who use lowballing—airlines are

masters of this tactic, too. They'll entice you with rock-bottom ticket prices, but the true cost of your trip comes with a wave of additional fees.

Step 1: The Budget Flight You find a flight advertised for $99. It's too good to pass up, so you start the booking process.

Step 2: The Extra Fees Suddenly, there's a $30 charge for checked bags, $15 to choose your seat, $20 for a meal, and $25 for priority boarding. By the time you've added up all these extras, your $99 flight is now $189.

Outcome: Once you've started booking, it's hard to turn back. The final price is much higher than you expected, but you've already invested time and effort, so you go through with it.

Why Lowballing Works?

Lowballing works because it takes advantage of our tendency to commit once we've started down a path. After saying yes to a deal—or an idea—it's much harder to back out, even when the costs go up. We feel trapped, like we've already invested too much to walk away. And that's exactly what the lowballer is counting on.

To avoid falling for this tactic, it's important to read the fine print, ask questions, and be ready to walk away if things start to feel off. Lowballing may seem like a minor trick at first, but it can leave you paying far more than you bargained for.

In a world full of tempting offers and hidden costs, knowing how to spot lowballing can help you stay one step ahead.

4. The Bait-and-Switch Trap

Have you ever been drawn in by a deal that seems too good to be true, only to find out there's a catch? That's the classic bait-and-switch tactic, where a tempting offer hooks you in, but once you're ready to commit, the deal mysteriously changes.

Suddenly, you're being nudged towards a pricier option, or you discover that the original product isn't available at all.
Let's take a closer look at how this sneaky trick works in everyday life—and even in relationships and politics.

Ex: The Out-of-Stock Gadget

One of the most common places you'll see bait-and-switch is in electronics stores. They might advertise the latest smartphone or laptop at an unbelievable price, but there's a twist.

Step 1: The Bait: An electronics store advertises a laptop for just $299. It sounds like a steal, so customers rush in, eager to snag the deal.

Step 2: The Switch: Once inside, customers are told that the $299 model is either sold out or has very basic features. Salespeople then guide them toward a more expensive model—perhaps $499—claiming it has better specifications and will be a much smarter purchase in the long run.

Outcome: Customers feel like the pricier option is the better choice, even though they originally came in for the cheaper model. The store gets its sale, but the customer ends up paying much more than expected.

Ex: The Disappearing online Deal

The bait-and-switch isn't just reserved for physical stores. Online retailers play this game too, often with the promise of an amazing deal that vanishes at checkout.

Step 1: The Bait: You see a designer handbag online for $50. Excited, you quickly click to purchase.
Step 2: The Switch: But as soon as you try to check out, you're told the bag is out of stock. The website then suggests similar bags for $150, emphasizing their superior quality and design.
Outcome: Caught up in the shopping mood, many customers go ahead and buy the pricier alternative, even though they were originally attracted by the lower price.

The Bait-and-Switch in Relationships

Bait-and-switch doesn't only happen in sales—it can happen in personal relationships, too. Sometimes, people put on their best behavior to win someone's heart, only to reveal a very different side once they've gained their trust.

Ex Initial Charm vs. True Intentions

Step 1: The Bait At the start of a relationship, one partner might be overwhelmingly loving, showering their significant other with gifts, attention, and affection.
Step 2: The Switch But once the relationship is established, the behavior changes. The gifts and affection stop, and the partner might become distant, controlling, or even manipulative. The initial charm was just a mask.
Outcome: The other partner feels confused and disappointed, realizing the person they fell for was not who they thought.

The Bait-and-Switch in Politics

Even in politics, bait-and-switch tactics are used to sway voters and gain power.

Grand Plans vs. Reality

Step 1: The Bait During an election campaign, a politician might make grand promises, such as cutting taxes, improving healthcare, or creating millions of new jobs. These promises are designed to win votes and seem very appealing.

Step 2: The Switch After the election, the politician announces that circumstances have changed—perhaps the economy won't allow for those tax cuts after all. The promises are watered down or abandoned altogether.

Outcome: Voters feel betrayed, realizing the policies they voted for won't be coming to life as expected.

Why Bait-and-Switch Works

The bait-and-switch tactic works because it taps into human psychology. Once someone has invested time, energy, or hope into getting something, it becomes much harder to walk away, even when the terms change. By the time the "switch" happens, the person is often too committed to turn back.

Whether in retail, relationships, or politics, bait-and-switch tactics rely on building trust with an attractive offer and then taking advantage of that trust to push something else. The best defense is awareness—recognizing when something seems too good to be true and staying cautious when the deal starts to shift.

5. Red Herring

Sometimes, when someone doesn't want to face a tough situation, they distract you with something else. This is called a red herring or misdirection tactic. It's like throwing a random clue into a mystery story to make you look the other way, so you miss what's really important. People use these tricks in relationships, politics, and even everyday life to avoid blame, shift focus, or cover up the truth.

In Relationships

In romantic relationships, red herring tactics are often used to avoid difficult conversations or to cover up bad behavior.

a) Avoiding Problems

When one partner wants to talk about a serious issue, the other partner changes the subject to avoid it. For instance you want to discuss feeling neglected, but your partner starts talking about the dishes not being done. By shifting the topic, they avoid addressing the real issue—your feelings.

b) Hiding Infidelity

When accused of cheating, one partner may try to turn the tables by blaming the other person for being too suspicious. You confront your partner about cheating, and instead of explaining, they say, "You're just being paranoid. It's your jealousy that's ruining us!" Now, instead of talking about cheating, the conversation is about your trust issues.

c) Gaslighting

One partner makes the other doubt their memory or perception to avoid telling the truth.For instance you find a suspicious message on their phone, but when you bring it up, your partner says, "You're imagining things again." Now you're questioning yourself, and the real issue is ignored.

In Politics

In politics, red herring tactics are used to distract from scandals, controversies, or failures.

a) Changing the Topic

A politician facing criticism shifts attention to something else, often a new issue.

A politician gets caught misusing campaign funds. Instead of addressing it, they suddenly focus on a hot-button topic like immigration, hoping to draw attention away from the scandal.

b) Blaming Others

Instead of taking responsibility, politicians blame someone else—previous leaders, other parties, or even outside forces. When a government is blamed for a bad economy, they might say, "It's the fault of the previous administration," or "It's because of global problems," instead of discussing their own role.

c) Creating Distractions

To hide a policy failure, politicians might bring up irrelevant but sensational issues to grab attention. During a political failure, a leader might stage a flashy public event or talk about a celebrity endorsement to shift focus away from the real problems.

Why It Matters?

Red herring tactics can be dangerous because they distract us from important truths. Whether it's in personal relationships, where someone dodges responsibility, or in politics, where leaders try to escape scandals, these tactics make it harder to see what's really going on.

Being aware of red herrings can help you avoid falling for them. If a conversation suddenly changes direction or if someone blames others when faced with a problem, it might be time to dig deeper and focus on the real issue.

6. Framing

Framing is like putting a picture in a special frame. The frame can make you focus on certain parts of the picture and ignore others. In communication, framing works the same way—it's about presenting information in a way that changes how people see and understand it. The way something is framed can completely change how we feel about it. Let's look at some examples of how framing works in everyday life.

Framing in Marketing

Businesses are experts at framing things in a way that makes them more appealing. They carefully choose words and labels to highlight the good and downplay the bad.

Ex 1: Fat-Free Snacks: Imagine seeing a snack labeled as "90% fat-free." That sounds healthy, right? But it's really just another way of saying "contains 10% fat." The first version makes us feel better because it focuses on the positive, even though both labels mean the same thing.

Ex 2: Special Deals: A store offers "Buy One, Get One Free" instead of saying "50% off each item." Both deals are the same, but "getting something free" feels more exciting than a simple discount. This is framing at work—it makes the deal seem better than it actually is.

Framing in Personal Interactions

People use framing in their daily conversations to make situations seem more positive or to avoid blame.

Ex 1: Apologizing Without Apologizing If someone is late to a meeting, instead of saying, "I'm sorry I'm late," they might say, "Thank you for your patience." This shifts the focus away from their mistake and makes it about gratitude instead of fault. It feels better for both people.

Ex 2: Negotiating a Raise In a job negotiation, instead of just asking for a raise, an employee might say, "Based on my contributions and market rates, I believe a salary adjustment is fair." By framing the request this way, they make it sound reasonable and well-deserved, rather than just asking for more money.

Framing in Parenting

Parents often use framing to encourage their kids to do chores without making it feel like a boring task.

Ex: Teaching Responsibility Instead of telling a child to "help out around the house," a parent might say, "Doing these chores helps you build responsibility and important life skills." This way, the child sees the chores as something that helps them grow, rather than just a job to do.

Framing in the Medical Field

Imagine you're sitting in a doctor's office, nervously awaiting the news about a life-saving surgery. The doctor looks at you and says, "There's a 10% chance you might not survive the procedure." That number hits hard. It's terrifying, and your mind immediately imagines the worst.

Now, imagine the same doctor saying, "You've got a 90% chance of surviving this surgery." Suddenly, the odds feel in your favor. There's hope, and you feel more confident about moving forward.

In cancer treatment, framing is often used when discussing the success rate of treatments. If a doctor says, "This treatment has a 70% survival rate," patients tend to feel optimistic. However, if the same doctor says, "There's a 30% chance of dying from this treatment," the patient may feel anxious and hopeless—even though the probability is exactly the same. Framing the information positively often helps patients make more confident, less fear-driven decisions.

Both statements convey the same information—one emphasizes the risk, while the other highlights the positive outcome. This is a classic example of framing, a powerful psychological tool used in communication, especially in the medical field. The way information is presented, even when the facts don't change, can drastically impact how a patient feels and the decisions they make.

Why Framing Matters

Framing is a powerful tool that can shape how we see and understand the world around us. Whether it's in marketing, personal conversations, or even historical movements, the way information is presented can influence how we feel and what decisions we make. By paying attention to framing, we can better understand the hidden intentions behind the information we're given and make more thoughtful choices. Understanding framing helps us see through the surface and think critically about what's really being said.

7. Emotional Appeals

Emotional appeals involve leveraging emotions like fear, guilt, or desire to influence decision-making or behavior. While they can be used ethically, their misuse can lead to manipulation and unethical outcomes, particularly in relationships and politics.

In Relationships

Imagine you're standing at a crossroads, not sure which path to take. You want to do what's right, but someone whispers in your ear, filling your mind with fear or desire. These whispers? They're emotional appeals—powerful tools that can gently nudge you in one direction or, at their worst, forcefully shove you down a path you never wanted.

Let's start with relationships. We all want love, security, and happiness, but sometimes emotions like fear, guilt, or desire can be twisted to control us.

Fear

Imagine two people who love each other, but one begins to subtly wield fear like a weapon. "If you ever leave me, no one else will love you like I do," they say. Suddenly, that love feels like a cage. The fear of loneliness, of never finding someone else, makes the other person stay. Not out of love anymore, but out of fear. It's a heartbreaking manipulation where one partner controls the other by making them believe they'll be lost without them.

Guilt

A partner might bring up past mistakes or sacrifices "After all I've done for you, how can you say no to this small favor?" It's as if the weight of their past kindness forces you into decisions you're not comfortable with. The manipulation is quiet but heavy, like carrying around a bag of stones, each one a reminder of how you "owe" them.

Desire

Desire can be the sweetest, most tempting tool. "If you really loved me, you'd quit your job and stay home with me." It sounds like love, but underneath, it's a trap. Your desire to please your partner, to show your love, becomes a way for them to control your life, to pull the strings without you even noticing.

Emotions at Play in Politics

Now, zoom out from the intimacy of relationships and look at the bigger picture—politics. The stakes are higher, and the audience is vast, but the emotional strings are the same.

Fear

Politicians often paint the future with dark, frightening colors. "If we don't pass this law, criminals will flood our streets," they declare, planting seeds of fear in every mind. Fear is a powerful motivator. It makes people agree to things they wouldn't normally, simply because they're too scared of the alternative. A famous example? The lead-up to the Iraq War. Fear of weapons of mass destruction was enough to convince the world to act, even when the facts were shaky.

Desire

Then comes the glittering promise of desire. "Elect me, and everyone will have high-paying jobs and free healthcare." It's the dream we all want, but often it's just that—a dream. These promises stir up hope, but too often, they're impossible to fulfill. Yet in the heat of desire, logic fades.

8. Social Proof

Imagine now that you're surrounded by people, and all of them seem to agree on something. It's hard to go against the crowd, right? This is the power of social proof—when the behavior or opinions of others shape what we think or do. It can be used for good, but it can also be used to manipulate us.

Peer Pressure in Relationships

In relationships, one partner might say, "All our friends think you should quit your job and stay home." Suddenly, it feels like the whole world is telling you what to do. You don't want to seem like the odd one out, so you start to question your own thoughts. Is this really what everyone thinks? The pressure grows, and before you know it, you're doubting yourself because you feel alone in your opinion.

Manipulating Perception

Some people go a step further. They might twist stories about your relationship, spreading half-truths or lies to friends and family. Suddenly, the people you'd normally turn to for advice start siding with the manipulative partner. "I heard you've been causing trouble," they might say, leaving you feeling isolated, misunderstood, and cornered.

False Consensus

A partner might claim, "Everyone fights like we do; it's normal." By making their behavior seem common, they make you question your own feelings. Maybe it *is* normal, you think. Maybe I'm overreacting. This false sense of consensus makes you stay in situations you're uncomfortable with because it feels like everyone else is doing the same.

Politics and the Crowd's Influence

In the political arena, social proof is like a magic trick. Politicians often try to make it seem like everyone's on their side, even if it's not true.

Astroturfing

Sometimes they create fake support through astroturfing—making it look like there's a groundswell of public backing when there really isn't. They might hire people to post positive comments or stage rallies, all to convince you that everyone else is on board. If the crowd supports them, shouldn't you?

Manipulating Polls

Then there's the manipulation of polls—cherry-picking data to show fake support for a policy or a candidate. It might seem like everyone loves this new law or leader, but behind the scenes, the numbers have been carefully arranged to make you believe a lie.

Media Endorsements

What about the media? In some cases, only positive stories make it through, giving the illusion that everything is rosy. During India's Emergency in the 1970s, the press was tightly controlled, and all you heard were the government's glowing reports. Anyone who disagreed was silenced, creating the false sense that the whole nation was in agreement.

9. Authority Figures

In today's world, celebrities and social media influencers hold incredible power over public opinion. They influence everything from what we wear to how we think. But here's the problem: just because someone is famous doesn't mean they're an expert on every topic. We often forget this because our brains are wired to trust authority figures—whether they're scientists, doctors, or movie stars.

Imagine this: you're scrolling through Instagram, and a popular influencer or celebrity you admire starts talking about a new political movement or endorses a skincare product that promises magical results, mental health or medical area. Because of their fame, charisma, or success in another field, it's easy to think they know what they're talking about—even when they might not. This is the cognitive bias of authority figures at play, where people trust and believe those in positions of perceived authority, even if their knowledge on a subject is questionable.

The Rise of Social Media Influencers

Platforms like Instagram, Youtube, Facebook, X and TikTok have turned regular people into authority figures. A fitness influencer might suddenly start offering diet advice, or a beauty guru may endorse a political candidate. Often, influencers promote products or ideologies not because they're experts but because they're paid to do so. Their endorsements, driven by sponsorships and partnerships, can distort their true opinions, making it hard for their audience to see the bias behind the promotion.

An example of this is the promotion of certain "detox teas" or weight loss supplements by influencers on Instagram. Many of these products have been criticized for being ineffective or harmful, yet influencers promote them because they're paid to do so. Their millions of followers, trusting their judgment, buy into these products without questioning the science behind them.

The Danger of Blind Trust

The biggest danger of the cognitive bias of authority figures is blind trust. When we assume that someone knows what they're talking about because they're famous or successful, we stop questioning the information they present. This can lead to misinformation spreading quickly and people making decisions based on poor advice, whether it's related to health, politics, or consumer products.

The key is to stay critical and aware. Just because someone is famous doesn't mean they're an expert on everything. We need to question endorsements, do our own research, and make informed decisions rather than blindly trusting influencers and celebrities.

10. Anchoring

Imagine you're about to make a decision, and someone throws out a number or idea that seems far too high, or maybe too low. At first, you dismiss it as unrealistic. But slowly, without even realizing it, that number or idea sticks in your mind and shapes how you think about the situation. This is anchoring—a clever, sometimes manipulative, technique where the first piece of information you receive becomes a reference point. That "anchor" influences everything that comes after, guiding your thoughts and decisions, even if the initial information wasn't fair or reasonable.

Anchoring in Real Life

Anchoring can show up in everyday situations, especially in relationships, politics, and sales, where people use it to subtly steer the decisions of others.

In Relationships

Anchoring can take a personal form, especially when one partner sets high or unrealistic expectations to influence the other. But the anchor has influenced how you think about love, duty, and what's "normal" in a relationship.

In Politics

Politicians know how to use anchoring to their advantage, often starting with extreme ideas to make less extreme ones seem more reasonable.

Policy Suggestions

Imagine a government proposing a 50% budget cut to a public program. The public outcry is immediate. But after protests and debates, the government "compromises" and reduces the cut to 20%. People breathe a sigh of relief, feeling like they've won. But what they don't realize is that the government never intended to cut the budget by 50%—the real plan was always 20%. The initial extreme proposal was the anchor, designed to make the final decision feel like a fair compromise, even though it's still a significant cut.

In Sales

Salespeople are experts at using anchoring to influence buyers, especially when it comes to negotiating prices.

The Used Car Dealership

Picture yourself at a used car dealership. You've got your eye on a car, and the dealer tells you it's priced at 5 lakhs. It feels like a steep price, so you start negotiating. After some back and forth, the dealer agrees to drop the price to 3.5 lakhs, and then knocks off another 50,000. You walk away thinking you've scored a great deal. But what you didn't realize is that 5 lakhs was never the real price—the dealer always intended to sell it for around 3 lakhs. That 5 lakh figure was an anchor, planted to make you feel like you were getting a bargain when, in reality, you paid what the dealer wanted all along.

Anchoring plays on our instinct to judge everything based on the first piece of information we receive. It tricks us into thinking we're making better decisions when, really, our judgment is being swayed.

11. Ambiguity

Ambiguity is like a fog that settles in, making everything unclear. When people use it, they rely on confusing or vague language to blur the lines between truth and deception. It's a clever trick because it allows them to dodge commitments, avoid responsibility, and control how things are understood without ever saying anything definite. This sneaky tactic shows up all the time, especially in relationships and politics. Let's dive into how ambiguity is used to manipulate and confuse.

In Relationships

Ambiguity can be a powerful weapon in personal relationships, where clarity and trust are key. Here's how it's often used to control or deceive

Avoiding Commitment

Imagine asking your partner about your future together, and they respond with, "Let's wait and see." It sounds like they're open to possibilities, but in reality, they're keeping things uncertain. By avoiding a clear answer, they leave you in limbo, unable to plan or make informed decisions. It's a way to stay non-committal without fully rejecting the idea, keeping you hooked without any promises.

Deflecting Responsibility

Have you ever heard, "I thought you understood," when someone didn't communicate clearly? This is another form of ambiguity. Instead of owning up to poor communication, they shift the blame onto you. It's not their fault—they assume you got it. This vague language allows them to avoid taking responsibility for their actions while making you feel like you're the one who misinterpreted things.

In Politics

Politicians are masters of ambiguity, often using it to appeal to everyone without committing to anything concrete. Here's how it plays out on the political stage

Vague Policies

Politicians love to talk about "better healthcare" or "stronger education systems," but what do those words really mean? Without specifics, it's hard to know what they're promising. By keeping things vague, they make it difficult to hold them accountable later on. People hear what they want to hear, but there's no clear plan in place.

Campaign Promises

During elections, politicians often make sweeping promises that sound good but lack detail. They might say, "I'll create more jobs," but without explaining how. This vague language lets them appeal to a wide audience because everyone can interpret the statement in a way that fits their needs. Later, if the promise isn't fulfilled, the lack of specifics gives them room to wiggle out of blame.

Evading Accountability

When things go wrong, politicians often rely on phrases like, "Mistakes were made." Who made the mistakes? What went wrong? The language is so unclear that it's hard to tell. By not being specific, they avoid taking personal responsibility and instead create confusion, making it difficult to hold anyone accountable.

12. Omission

Omission is a silent form of manipulation, where crucial information is deliberately withheld. It can create misleading impressions and steer others in a direction that suits the person leaving out the details. This tactic is subtle but powerful, and when used unethically, it can cause significant harm, especially in personal relationships and politics. Let's explore how omission works in real life and the damage it can cause when important truths are hidden.

Omission in Relationships

In personal relationships, trust is everything. But when one person withholds important details, it's like building a house on shaky ground. It may seem stable at first, but when the truth comes out, everything can come crashing down. Here's how omission can quietly destroy trust

Hiding Past Relationships

Imagine being in a relationship where one partner doesn't disclose a past romantic relationship with a mutual friend. At first, it may seem harmless, but when the truth eventually surfaces, it can lead to feelings of betrayal. The omitted information creates doubt—what else might they be hiding? This kind of omission plants seeds of mistrust that can grow into bigger issues over time.

Concealing Financial Troubles

Money is a major factor in many relationships, and financial transparency is key. But what happens when one partner hides significant debts or financial struggles? Maybe they've maxed out credit cards or taken out loans without telling their partner. When the truth finally comes to light, the financial strain isn't the only problem. The real damage comes from the breach of trust, leaving the other partner feeling deceived and blindsided.

Not Mentioning Health Conditions

Imagine a partner withholding information about a serious health condition, like a sexually transmitted infection (STI). This is more than just a personal matter—it can put the other partner's health at risk. Discovering such a crucial fact after the fact creates serious ethical concerns and can shatter the foundation of trust in the relationship.

Omission in Politics

Just like in relationships, omission in politics can have devastating effects, but on a much larger scale. Citizens rely on complete and accurate information to make informed decisions about their leaders and policies. When key facts are left out, it erodes public trust and undermines democracy itself.

Vague Promises and Policies

Politicians sometimes omit important details from their speeches or policy proposals. They might promise better healthcare or job opportunities, but fail to explain how they plan to deliver. By leaving out critical information, they avoid being held accountable if things don't turn out as promised. This lack of transparency makes it harder for people to trust their leaders.

Shifting the Blame

When something goes wrong, omission can be a tool to dodge

responsibility. Instead of owning up to mistakes, politicians might focus on external factors—natural disasters, economic downturns, or even the actions of other governments—while quietly leaving out the role their own policies played. This selective storytelling keeps the public from seeing the full picture and delays real solutions.

In politics, omission is a way to control the narrative. By withholding key information, politicians can manipulate public perception, avoid accountability, and mislead citizens. It's a tactic that erodes trust in leadership and makes it difficult for people to make well-informed choices.

13. Half-Truths and Selective Disclosure

Half-truths and selective disclosure are subtle but powerful ways of manipulating others. By mixing a little truth with what's left unsaid, these tactics can distort reality, influencing how people think and make decisions. Whether in relationships or politics, the effects of these deceptive practices can be far-reaching, leading to confusion, mistrust, and even tragedy. Let's dive into how this works in real life.

Half-Truths in Relationships

In relationships, half-truths can tear down trust, creating a fog of uncertainty. When someone shares only part of the truth, they control the story, making it hard to know what's real. Here's how half-truths are used unethically in personal relationships

Infidelity

A partner might say, "I was out with friends," which is technically true—but what they don't mention is that they were also meeting someone they're romantically involved with. By omitting this critical detail, they give a misleading impression of their whereabouts, making it seem like nothing is wrong when, in reality, they're hiding their unfaithfulness.

Financial Deception

Another example One partner claims, "I've paid off a significant part of the debt." This might be true, but they conveniently leave out the fact that they've also taken on new debts. By sharing just enough of the truth, they create the false impression that they're being financially responsible, when in fact, the situation is much worse.

Half-Truths in Politics

Half-truths are a favorite tool in politics, allowing leaders to shape public perception while hiding inconvenient facts. Here's how politicians use half-truths to manipulate the truth while maintaining a veneer of honesty

Economic Statistics

Imagine a politician proudly announcing, "Unemployment has decreased by 5%!" While this might be factually true, what they fail to mention is that the decrease is largely due to an increase in low-wage, part-time jobs rather than sustainable full-time employment. This half-truth paints a rosy picture of the economy, hiding the reality that many people are still struggling.

Education Funding

Another common tactic "We have increased funding for education!" This may sound like good news, but the leader conveniently leaves out the fact that the increase is minimal and doesn't account for inflation or rising student enrollment. It's technically true, but the full picture is far less impressive.

Crisis Management

During a disaster or crisis, governments might highlight successful evacuation efforts while neglecting to mention those left behind or areas where their response failed. By sharing only the positive aspects of their actions, they create the impression of competence while concealing the true scale of the problem. In politics, half-truths allow leaders to present themselves as successful and trustworthy, even when the reality is much more complex. The result? A public that believes in a distorted version of the truth.

14. False Dilemma

Imagine you're standing at a crossroads, and someone tells you there are only two paths you can take. You feel trapped, forced to choose between two extremes, but what if there were more roads, hidden just out of sight? This is the essence of a false dilemma—a manipulative trick where a situation is presented as having only two opposing options, when in reality, other alternatives exist. It's a way to limit choices, push decisions, and control outcomes. Let's explore how this sneaky tactic shows up in real life, in both personal relationships and politics.

False Dilemma in Relationships

In relationships, the false dilemma can be used to corner someone into making a decision by making it seem like there are only two options—when in truth, many more solutions might exist. Here's how it plays out

Ultimatums

A partner might say, "Either you quit your job, or our relationship is over." At first glance, it looks like a clear-cut decision either choose the relationship or the career. But this is a false choice. It ignores the possibility of compromise—perhaps finding ways to balance work and relationship or having an open conversation about why the job is an issue. The ultimatum forces the partner to pick one extreme, leaving no room for discussion.

Parenting Decisions

Imagine one parent telling the other, "We either send our child to this specific school, or we don't care about their education." This statement sets up a false dilemma choose the school or be labeled as neglectful. But this ignores the fact that there are likely many schools that could offer a great education, and perhaps other factors need to be considered. It's a manipulative way of pushing a decision by making the other parent feel guilty or pressured.

Time Together

A common false dilemma in relationships is, "You either spend all your free time with me, or you don't love me." This frames the situation as all or nothing—total devotion or no love at all. But relationships thrive on balance, and healthy boundaries are important. The idea that love can only be proven by giving up all your personal time is a misleading and harmful way to frame the relationship.

False Dilemma in Politics

In politics, the false dilemma is often used to polarize issues, forcing people to pick sides without considering alternative solutions. It's a powerful tool to manipulate public opinion and simplify complex issues into black-and-white choices. Here's how it works

Economic Policies

A politician might declare, "We either cut taxes or destroy the economy." This statement suggests that tax cuts are the only solution to economic problems, but it ignores other options, like reforming the tax system, investing in infrastructure, or focusing on job creation. By presenting just two options—cut taxes or face disaster—the politician narrows the debate and pressures people into supporting their view.

National Security

During debates on security, a leader might say, "We either increase surveillance, or we face constant terrorist threats." This argument pushes the idea that the only way to ensure safety is through more surveillance, ignoring other possibilities like strengthening intelligence services, improving international cooperation, or addressing root causes of terrorism. It's a tactic designed to make people feel like they have no choice but to give up privacy for security.

Healthcare Reform

Ex: A political figure might argue, "You either support this healthcare bill, or you don't care about people's health." This frames the debate as a choice between one specific bill and complete indifference to healthcare. But the truth is, there are likely many different ways to approach healthcare reform, and opposing one bill doesn't mean someone doesn't care. The false dilemma simplifies a complex issue and pressures people into making a decision based on fear or guilt.

15. Misleading Statistics

Imagine you're trying to prove your point in a debate or argument, but instead of presenting the full picture, you only choose the bits of information that make you look good. That's cherry-picking—choosing only the facts that support your side, while ignoring the rest. It's like telling half the story, but making it seem like the whole truth.

Cherry-picking often goes hand in hand with another tactic using misleading statistics. Here's how this combination plays out in marketing, health, education, and more.

a) Selective Testimonials

Companies love to show off glowing reviews. A skincare brand might say, "90% of users saw an improvement in their skin!" But what they don't tell you is that this figure comes from a tiny group of customers, or that many others didn't see any changes—or worse, had side effects. By highlighting just the positive experiences, they create a false impression of the product's effectiveness.

b) Selective Health Claims

Ever seen those flashy ads for supplements? "Our product boosts energy by 50%!" they claim. But this might be based on a small, short-term study that doesn't reflect the full story. Other research might show no real benefit at all, but by cherry-picking favorable data, the company makes you think their product is a miracle cure.

c) Test Scores in Schools

Schools can also play the cherry-picking game. A school might proudly announce, "Our students scored 20% above the national average in math!" What they don't tell you is that they're only talking about a select group of students, ignoring others who didn't do as well, or subjects where scores were much lower. This selective reporting makes the school seem better than it is.

d) Selective Nutritional Benefits

Food companies are masters at cherry-picking when it comes to nutrition. A cereal brand might boast, "Our cereal is high in fiber!" What they leave out is that the same cereal is loaded with sugar and artificial additives. By shining a light only on the good stuff, they lead consumers to think the cereal is a healthy choice, when in reality, it might not be.

e) Team Performance Stats

Sports teams often highlight only their best performances. A team might say, "We've won 80% of our games this season!" But what they don't mention is that most of those wins were against weaker opponents, while they lost to the stronger teams. By picking and choosing their stats, they make their performance seem more impressive than it actually is.

16. Projection

Projection happens when a person subconsciously denies their own flaws or mistakes and places those same flaws onto someone else. It's like carrying around your own emotional baggage and handing it off to the nearest person, making them carry it instead.

In simple terms, when people feel uncomfortable with their feelings or actions, they accuse others of having those same traits to deflect attention away from themselves.

Imagine you're at work, and your colleague, Sarah, has a reputation for being disorganized. One day, a big project deadline is missed, and instead of admitting she dropped the ball, Sarah points fingers at you and others, accusing everyone else of being unorganized. The irony? Sarah is the one who's guilty of the very thing she's accusing others of. This is a classic example of projection, a common psychological manipulation tactic.

Projection in Relationships

Projection is especially common in relationships. For example, imagine a partner who's feeling insecure because they've been flirting with someone else. Instead of dealing with their guilt, they accuse you of flirting. Suddenly, you're on the defensive, trying to prove your innocence while the real problem—their unfaithfulness—goes unchecked.

Political Projection

We see projection even in politics. A leader may accuse the opposition of corruption when, in reality, they are the ones guilty of corrupt practices. This tactic shifts the conversation, so people forget to look at the accuser's own wrongdoings.

Why Do People Use Projection?

Projection is often a defence mechanism. It protects the ego from uncomfortable truths. When someone projects, they are avoiding the pain of confronting their own flaws. Instead, they force others to wear their guilt, shame, or insecurities.

17. Lying by Statistics

In an age where data is king, we tend to trust numbers blindly. After all, numbers are objective, right? They don't lie, they just state facts. But what if I told you that even statistics can be manipulated? Welcome to the world of "lying by statistics"—a subtle art where numbers are used to distort the truth rather than reveal it.

The Magic of the Misleading Average

Imagine you're looking for a new job and the recruiter proudly tells you that their company pays an *average* salary of $100,000 a year. Sounds fantastic, doesn't it? What they don't tell you is that the company CEO earns $1 million, while most employees make around $40,000. In this case, the *average* (or mean) salary is heavily skewed by one high earner at the top. The *median* salary, which is the midpoint of all salaries, would paint a much clearer picture of what most people actually earn, but that's not the number you're being shown.

Marketing Manipulation "Up to 50% Off!"

Have you ever seen an advertisement screaming "Up to 50% off!"? It makes you think you're about to save a ton of money, right? Well, not so fast. "Up to" means that only one or two items might be discounted by 50%, while most others are marked down by a mere 5 % or less. By choosing the most appealing number, marketers present a statistical illusion that draws you in without revealing the full story.

The Diet Pill Trap

Let's say you're watching late-night TV, and a flashy commercial comes on promoting a new weight-loss pill. The spokesperson claims, "In a study, 80% of participants lost weight!" That sounds great, but there's a hidden trick here. How many people were in the study? How much weight did they lose? Was the study done in a week or a year? What the commercial doesn't mention is that the "study" might have involved only five people, two of whom dropped out, and the weight loss could have been just a pound or two. By cherry-picking the most favorable statistic, the company hides the lackluster reality behind an impressive-sounding number.

The Art of Statistical Spin

In politics, numbers can be twisted to sway public opinion. During election campaigns, candidates often boast, "Unemployment dropped by 5% during my term!" But what does that really mean? Did people find better jobs or were they forced to take low-wage, part-time work? Are they no longer counted in the unemployment statistics because they've given up looking for a job entirely? Politicians often spin statistics in ways that highlight their achievements, but closer inspection reveals the reality isn't always so rosy.

The "Small Sample Size" Trick

You've probably seen headlines like "Drinking coffee reduces the risk of heart disease by 25%!" But wait—how many people participated in this study? If it was a small group of 20 people, then the findings aren't all that reliable. Small sample sizes can lead to large, misleading variations in results. The headline might be true for the specific group, but it doesn't necessarily apply to the general population. However, the dramatic number catches attention and makes for a compelling, albeit deceptive, story.

18. Survivorship bias

Survivorship Bias occurs when we focus only on the "survivors" or successes in a particular group while ignoring the failures that didn't make it. In other words, we see the winners and assume their path to success is typical, forgetting about the countless others who followed the same path but didn't succeed.

Self-Help Industry

The self-help industry thrives on stories of people who succeeded by adopting specific habits, routines, or mindsets. It's easy to find books or seminars that showcase examples of people who followed a certain strategy and went on to achieve incredible success. But what about the countless people who followed the same advice and failed?

For example, consider the stories of famous entrepreneurs like Steve Jobs or Elon Musk. They are often highlighted as examples of people who took massive risks and made it big. But what's often left out are the stories of the thousands of entrepreneurs who took similar risks and didn't succeed. The failure rate for startups is staggeringly high, yet books and motivational speakers typically focus on the rare few who made it through the challenging road.

One common piece of advice in self-help is the idea of "never giving up." While persistence is important, survivorship bias ignores the reality that many people who persist still fail. We tend to hear about the ones who made it, reinforcing the idea that hard work and determination guarantee success. In reality, success often requires more than just grit—it involves timing, luck, connections, and many factors outside one's control.

Fitness and Diet Industries

The fitness industry is another arena where survivorship bias is rampant. Think of the many weight-loss success stories promoted by fitness programs or diet plans. Companies highlight the people who lost significant weight and transformed their lives, but they rarely mention those who followed the same program and didn't see results.

For example, social media influencers or celebrities often showcase their amazing body transformations, crediting a particular workout routine or diet. What they don't show are the hundreds or thousands of people who tried the same approach and failed to achieve those results due to factors like genetics, metabolism, or lifestyle.

Survivorship Bias in Other Areas

Investing: Survivorship bias can also skew our perceptions in finance. When we hear about people who made fortunes through stock market investments or cryptocurrencies, we tend to believe that these are common outcomes. We don't hear as often about those who lost money or failed because they followed the same strategies but were less lucky.

Education and Careers: In education, we're told that graduates from top schools or certain degrees go on to lead successful careers. But we often overlook the fact that many people from these schools or with these degrees struggle to find jobs or end up in fields unrelated to their studies.

War Heroes and Historical Figures: The stories of war heroes or historical figures who changed the world often ignore the countless people who tried to do the same and were either forgotten or faced disastrous consequences.

Dotcom Bubble

The dotcom bubble of the late 1990s is a prime example of survivorship bias in action. During this period, many internet-based companies launched, and some became wildly successful, like Amazon and Google. These companies are often cited as examples of how the internet boom was a golden opportunity for anyone willing to take a chance. However, we rarely hear about the thousands of dotcom companies that crashed and burned during that same time. People remember the survivors, not the failures, which can lead to an inflated sense of how easy it was to succeed during the internet boom.

Survivorship bias is a powerful cognitive trap that affects how we view success in every aspect of life, from business to fitness to self-improvement. It's important to remember that for every success story, there are countless others who didn't make it. Recognizing this bias can help us set more realistic expectations and make better-informed decisions, whether we're reading self-help books, starting a business, or embarking on a new fitness journey. The key is not to be discouraged by the failures but to understand that success stories often leave out a big part of the picture.

19. Obfuscation and Sophistry

Obfuscation is the deliberate act of making something unclear or difficult to understand. It's like covering the truth with layers of confusion so that people can't see what's really going on. In politics and religion, obfuscation can be used to dodge accountability, avoid answering direct questions, or distract people from uncomfortable truths.

Imagine a debate where the person on the stage isn't really answering the questions. Instead, they're twisting words, speaking in circles, or using overly complicated language to confuse everyone listening. You feel like something important is being said, but the more you listen, the less clear things become. This is the art of obfuscation and sophistry, tools often used in politics and religion to manipulate and deceive.

What is Sophistry?

Sophistry is the use of clever but misleading arguments. Sophists, in ancient Greece, were known for using rhetoric and persuasion to win arguments rather than seeking the truth. Today, this technique is often used to convince people of something that may sound logical but is actually flawed or deceptive.

These tactics go hand in hand in both politics and religion, where the goal is often not to clarify or seek truth but to persuade, manipulate, or maintain power.

Politics and the Power of Obfuscation

In politics, obfuscation is commonly used when politicians want to evade tough questions or hide the real intent behind their actions. They may give long, convoluted answers that confuse the audience or use technical jargon to throw off critics.

Ex: During press conferences or political debates, you might hear a politician being asked about a controversial decision. Instead of providing a clear answer, they might launch into a speech about unrelated topics, citing economic data or historical examples that don't directly address the issue. The aim is to distract and confuse the public, leaving people unsure about the real answer.

Sophistry in Religion

In religious contexts, sophistry is often used to justify or defend controversial doctrines. Religious leaders may employ these tactics to maintain power or sway followers by appealing to emotions rather than reason. Sometimes, they use rhetoric to make their arguments appear irrefutable, even though the logic may be weak or circular.

It's important to stay vigilant, question overly complicated or emotionally charged arguments, and seek out the underlying facts. The more we can see through obfuscation and sophistry, the better we can resist being manipulated and make informed decisions. The key to overcoming these tactics is education, critical thinking, and transparency.

20. Confirmation Bias and Groupthink

Our minds play tricks on us. Confirmation bias and groupthink are two ways this happens, shaping how we make decisions, form opinions, and relate to others. Confirmation bias is when we only seek information that supports what we already believe, while ignoring or dismissing anything that challenges it.

Groupthink, on the other hand, is when we go along with the majority opinion to avoid standing out, even if we have doubts. These mental habits can impact everything from politics to family dynamics, often leading to bad decisions and missed opportunities for open thinking.

In Politics

Searching for Support, Ignoring the Science

In the ongoing debate over climate change, confirmation bias plays a big role. Imagine someone who believes that climate change is a hoax. Instead of listening to experts or reading reports from trusted organizations like the Intergovernmental Panel on Climate Change (IPCC), they search for articles from questionable websites or listen to non-experts who say what they want to hear. They may even brush aside overwhelming scientific evidence as "fake news" or conspiracy. This way of cherry-picking information strengthens their belief and shuts down any chance of meaningful discussion or policy action on the issue.

Seeing Only What You Want to See

Confirmation bias also influences how people view elections. Supporters of a particular candidate might only watch news channels or read articles that praise their favorite, completely ignoring negative reports or critical polls. They surround themselves with positive coverage, dismissing anything unfavorable as biased or false. This creates an "echo chamber" where their belief in the candidate's success gets stronger, no matter what the actual facts or results say. They end up living in a bubble, convinced they're right and everyone else is wrong.

In Relationships

You Only See the Bad

Relationships can be tricky, and confirmation bias can make things worse, especially when trust is involved. Imagine one partner who already thinks the other can't be trusted. Every small inconsistency, missed call, or unexplained delay is seen as proof of dishonesty. Positive actions, like being open or making an effort, are ignored. This kind of biased thinking creates a cycle of suspicion and conflict, where the partner's belief in the other's untrustworthiness gets stronger and harder to break, even if it's not true.

Only Seeing One Side

Parents often experience confirmation bias when it comes to making decisions about how to raise their children. For example, a parent who believes in strict discipline might only read books, articles, or studies that support this approach. They might dismiss any research suggesting that a more lenient or flexible style could be better for the child's emotional well-being. By focusing on only one viewpoint, the parent may miss out on valuable insights that could lead to a healthier, more balanced approach to parenting.

Groupthink in Politics

Bay of Pigs Invasion

One of the most famous examples of groupthink in politics is the Bay of Pigs invasion in 1961. President John F. Kennedy and his advisors planned to invade Cuba and overthrow Fidel Castro. Some of Kennedy's advisors had serious doubts, but the pressure to agree with the group was too strong. No one wanted to stand out or create conflict. As a result, the group moved forward with the plan, which ended in disaster. This failure showed how groupthink can lead to poor decisions when people don't feel comfortable voicing concerns.

21. Slippery Slope Fallacy

The slippery slope fallacy is a sneaky way of arguing, suggesting that if we take one small step in a certain direction, it will lead to a chain of events—usually bad ones—that are supposedly inevitable. But the problem with this argument is that it jumps to extreme conclusions without any solid proof. You often see this tactic in politics and relationships, where it's used to scare or persuade people to avoid certain actions. Let's dive into some real-life examples to see how this fallacy plays out.

In Politics

Gun Control Laws

Scenario: In the United States, the debate over gun control often brings out slippery slope arguments.

Argument: "If we allow background checks on gun purchases, soon the government will confiscate all firearms and leave the entire population defenseless."

Analysis: This argument leaps from a sensible, limited step (background checks) to an extreme and unfounded fear (total disarmament). There's no evidence that one leads to the other. The argument works by feeding on fear, not by presenting facts or a logical chain of events.

Healthcare Reform

Scenario: When discussing government involvement in healthcare, opponents often use the slippery slope fallacy to argue against it.

Argument: "If we let the government offer universal healthcare, we'll end up with full-blown socialism and the destruction of free-market capitalism."

Analysis: This argument paints a grim picture, suggesting that one policy change (universal healthcare) will eventually spiral into a completely different economic system. It overlooks the reality that policies are complex, and there are many checks and balances to prevent such extreme outcomes. This argument thrives on exaggeration rather than reality.

In Relationships

Trust and Independence

Scenario: Imagine one partner asking for a bit more personal space in a relationship, like spending time with friends.

Argument: "If I let you go out with your friends without me, soon you'll want to spend every weekend away, and eventually, you'll leave me."

Analysis: This argument makes a giant leap from allowing a partner some freedom to predicting the end of the relationship. It assumes that small, reasonable actions—like hanging out with friends—will automatically lead to a worst-case scenario. Instead of trusting the relationship's strength, this argument gives in to exaggerated fears.

Conflict Resolution

Scenario: During a disagreement, one partner might resist compromise by using a slippery slope argument.

Argument: "If I change my work schedule this time to suit you, you'll always expect me to prioritize your needs, and I'll lose my independence."

Analysis: Here, a simple compromise (changing a work schedule) is blown out of proportion, making it seem like a one-time favor will result in a complete loss of personal autonomy. It ignores the fact that relationships thrive on balance, and compromises can be made without one person giving up everything.

The slippery slope fallacy taps into people's fears of what *might* happen if a certain action is taken, no matter how unrealistic or exaggerated those fears may be. In politics, it's often used to stir up public opposition to policies by predicting an exaggerated, negative future. In relationships, it can create unnecessary tension, assuming small changes or compromises will lead to extreme consequences. Recognizing this fallacy helps us focus on rational discussions and make decisions based on facts rather than fears.

22. Circular Reasoning

Circular reasoning, also called "begging the question," is another tricky argument style where the conclusion is simply restated as its own proof. Instead of offering real evidence, the argument goes around in a circle, assuming that the conclusion is already correct. Let's break down some examples from politics and relationships to see how circular reasoning works.

In Politics

Scenario: A politician claims they are the best candidate for a leadership role.
Argument: "I am the best candidate for president because I'm the most qualified. How do we know I'm the most qualified? Because I'm running for president!"
Analysis: This argument is a perfect loop. It doesn't give any evidence to show why the candidate is qualified; it just keeps repeating the claim that they're the best without providing any real proof. It tricks the listener into thinking there's support for the conclusion, but in reality, it's just restating the claim in different words.

Policy Effectiveness

Scenario: During debates about a new policy, supporters might use circular reasoning to defend it.

Argument: "This education policy is working because it improves education. How do we know it improves education? Because it's a successful policy!"

Analysis: This argument doesn't provide any actual evidence to show that the policy is effective. Instead, it simply repeats the conclusion (it's successful) as its own proof, creating a circle that doesn't offer real data or analysis.

In Relationships

Ex 1: Trust Issues

Scenario: One partner accuses the other of being untrustworthy without solid evidence.

Argument: "You are untrustworthy because I can't trust you. And I can't trust you because you are untrustworthy."

Analysis: This argument goes around in circles, offering no actual proof of untrustworthiness. It assumes that trust is broken without pointing to any specific reason, making it impossible to address the real issue. It's a loop that traps both partners in a never-ending cycle of mistrust.

Justifying Behavior

Scenario: During an argument, one partner tries to justify their behavior by using circular reasoning.

Argument: "I'm right to be upset because my feelings are always justified. And my feelings are always justified because I'm right to be upset."

Analysis: This argument offers no real reason why the partner's feelings are justified in this particular situation. Instead, it creates a loop where the person's emotions are treated as self-evident, blocking any chance for meaningful discussion or resolution.

In Politics

Scenario: Indian political leaders sometimes make bold statements about their qualifications using circular reasoning.

Argument: "I am the best choice for Prime Minister because I'm the most capable leader. And I'm the most capable leader because I'm the best choice for Prime Minister."

Analysis: This is a classic case of circular reasoning, where the leader assumes their capability without giving real evidence or accomplishments. The argument goes in a circle, repeating the same point without offering solid proof.

Family Expectations

Scenario: In Indian families, parents might justify their expectations for their children's careers through circular reasoning.

Argument: "You must become a doctor because it's the best career for you. How do we know it's the best career for you? Because it's what we expect you to do."

Analysis: This reasoning uses the parents' expectation as the only proof that becoming a doctor is the right choice, ignoring the child's interests or abilities. It's a closed loop that doesn't allow for discussion or consideration of other options.

Circular reasoning can make weak arguments sound strong by repeating the conclusion as its own proof. In politics, it can be used to push a point without providing real evidence, while in relationships, it can lead to misunderstandings and unresolved conflicts. By recognizing circular reasoning, we can break free from these endless loops and focus on real, constructive discussions based on evidence and logic.

23. Post Hoc Ergo Propter Hoc

There's a sneaky little trap in our thinking called the "Post Hoc Ergo Propter Hoc" fallacy. It's Latin for "after this, therefore because of this." Basically, it's when we mistakenly believe that just because one thing happens after another, the first event must have caused the second. This kind of thinking can oversimplify things, ignoring other causes and overlooking the real complexity of life. Let's dive into examples from politics and relationships to see how this fallacy plays out.

Economic Policies

Scenario: A government rolls out a new economic policy, and soon after, the economy begins to grow.

Argument: "The economy grew after we introduced this policy, so the policy must have caused the growth."

Analysis: This argument jumps to conclusions, assuming the policy was the sole reason for the economic growth. But what about other factors like global market trends, technological advances, or the influence of previous policies? Could the growth have been a coincidence? It's easy to overlook these other possibilities and assume a direct cause and effect where none exists.

Crime Rates

Scenario: A new mayor takes office, and within a few months, the crime rate drops.

Argument: "Crime rates fell after the new mayor took office, so it must be because of their policies."

Analysis: Assuming the new mayor's actions directly caused the crime drop is tempting, but we miss out on so much more by thinking this way. Crime rates can shift for many reasons—seasonal changes, previous policies, or economic factors, for example. Maybe the mayor helped, but it's unlikely their leadership alone was responsible for the change.

In Relationships

Scenario: A couple starts arguing more frequently right after one partner begins a stressful new job.
Argument: "Our arguments started after you took this job, so your job must be causing our fights."
Analysis: While job stress might be playing a part, assuming it's the only reason ignores other possible causes like pre-existing relationship issues, communication problems, or even unrelated stresses. The new job could be adding fuel to the fire, but the fire might have already been there.

Changes in Behavior

Scenario: One partner becomes distant after they start spending more time with friends.
Argument: "You've been distant ever since you started hanging out with your friends more, so that must be why you're acting this way."
Analysis: It's easy to think that the increased time with friends is causing the distance. But maybe there are deeper issues at play—personal struggles, feelings of neglect, or unrelated stresses. Just because one thing happened after another doesn't mean one caused the other.

Changes in Health and Diet

Scenario: A person starts a new diet and shortly after, begins feeling more energetic.
Argument: "I feel more energetic after starting this diet, so the diet must be the reason for my improved energy."
Analysis: The diet might help, but assuming it's the only reason overlooks factors like better sleep, reduced stress, or

starting an exercise routine. Sometimes, it's the combination of several changes that lead to improvement, not just the diet alone.

Indian Social Contexts

Superstitions and Outcomes

Scenario: After performing a religious ritual, a family member gets a job promotion.

Argument: "The promotion happened after we performed the ritual, so the ritual caused the promotion."

Analysis: It's comforting to believe the ritual brought the good news, but factors like work performance, timing, or company needs are more likely explanations. The ritual might have given hope, but the promotion was probably due to professional merit.

The "Post Hoc Ergo Propter Hoc" fallacy simplifies complicated situations, making it seem like if one thing happens after another, the first must have caused the second. In politics, this can lead to incorrect conclusions about why policies succeed or fail. In relationships, it can cause misunderstandings and misplaced blame. Recognizing this fallacy helps us dig deeper into what might really be causing an outcome, leading to better decisions and clearer communication, whether in public life or personal relationships.

24. Hindsight Bias

Hindsight bias sneaks into our minds after something has happened, making us feel like we always knew the outcome—even if there was no way to predict it beforehand. This false sense of certainty can cloud our understanding of the past and impact our decisions for the future. Let's explore how this bias shows up in both politics and relationships.

In Politics

Election Outcomes

Scenario: A political analyst claims they knew the outcome of a tight election.

Argument: "I always knew Candidate X would win because of their strong social media presence and grassroots support."

Analysis: This is hindsight bias at work. Predicting the winner of a close election is rarely that simple. Before the results, the landscape was uncertain, with many factors at play. But now, knowing the outcome, the analyst confidently believes they could have seen it all along, ignoring the unpredictability of the election campaign.

Economic Crises

Scenario: After a financial crisis, economists and policymakers claim the warning signs were obvious.

Argument: "It was clear that the housing market would crash, given the rapid rise in home prices and risky lending."

Analysis: While some signs were there, the exact timing and scale of the crisis were hard to predict. Before the collapse, many experts didn't foresee the disaster coming. Hindsight bias now makes people believe they should have known all along, even though the economy's complexity often masks such outcomes.

In Relationships

Scenario: After a breakup, one partner says they always knew it wouldn't last.

Argument: "I knew from the start we weren't compatible and that the relationship would fail."

Analysis: This overlooks the good times and the genuine efforts made during the relationship. In reality, it wasn't always so clear. Hindsight bias makes the breakup seem inevitable, but at the time, the future was uncertain, and the outcome was far from obvious.

Handling Conflicts

Scenario: After resolving a big conflict, one partner believes they always knew the solution.

Argument: "I always knew that talking openly would solve our problems."

Analysis: While communication often helps, thinking that it was always the obvious solution is hindsight bias. In the heat of the conflict, many options might have been considered, and no one could be sure what would work. Now that it's over, the answer feels obvious, but it wasn't so clear when the conflict was unresolved.

Now let's look at how hindsight bias can influence perceptions in Indian politics and relationships.

Marriage Conflicts

Scenario: After years of marital tension, a couple divorces, and one partner claims they always knew it was coming.

Argument: "I knew we weren't right for each other from the beginning."

Analysis: Hindsight bias clouds the reality that relationships often evolve, with good times mixed in with challenges. While the breakup feels inevitable now, there were likely moments of hope and happiness. At the time, the future wasn't as clear as it seems in hindsight.

Hindsight bias makes us overconfident about predicting outcomes, giving us a skewed understanding of past events. In politics, this bias can make election results, economic crises, or policy decisions seem obvious after the fact, leading us to trust strategies or leaders without appreciating the complexities involved. In relationships, hindsight bias can reshape how we interpret conflicts or breakups, making us feel like we always knew how things would turn out—even when that wasn't the case.

By recognizing hindsight bias, we can maintain a more realistic view of the past, helping us learn more effectively and make better decisions in both public and personal life.

25. The Illusion of Control

The illusion of control is a trick our minds play on us, making us think we have more power over outcomes than we really do. It's a comforting thought, but it often misguides how we make decisions in both politics and relationships. Let's dive into some examples that show how this mindset can lead us astray.

In Politics

Election Campaigns

Picture this a candidate working tirelessly, shaking hands, making speeches, and rallying their supporters. They're confident that their effort will guarantee a win.

Claim: "I'm sure my campaign efforts will guarantee I win this election."

Insight: While a strong campaign is vital, election results depend on many other factors—voter preferences, party support, media influence, and sometimes even unforeseen events. The candidate's belief that their work alone will lead to victory reveals the illusion of control. They're missing the bigger picture elections are unpredictable, and not everything is within their grasp.

Economic Policies

Now, imagine a government rolling out a shiny new economic policy with grand promises. They believe this one policy will fix all the country's problems.

Claim: "This new tax reform will fix the economy and eliminate unemployment."

Insight: Economic outcomes are shaped by countless variables—global markets, technological advancements, even consumer behavior. Thinking that one policy will magically solve deep-rooted issues is a perfect example of the illusion of control. The government's optimism may overlook how unpredictable the economy can be, and how solving one problem often creates another.

In Relationships

Changing a Partner's Behavior

Think of a partner who believes they can get their significant other to kick a bad habit, like smoking or skipping exercise, just by encouraging them enough.

Claim: "If I keep encouraging you, I know I can get you to quit smoking and exercise."

Insight: While support is important, true change has to come from the individual. Believing that you can single-handedly change someone else's behavior is the illusion of control at play. It ignores the fact that personal habits are deeply rooted, and change depends on their willpower, not just your efforts.

Conflict Resolution

During a heated argument, one partner believes they can solve all the issues on their own, just by saying the right things or working harder to smooth things over.

Claim: "I can fix our problems if I just try hard enough and say the right things."

Insight: Resolving conflicts requires cooperation and understanding from both sides. Thinking you can handle everything alone is the illusion of control—it ignores the complexity of relationships, where both people need to be involved in finding a solution. No one has full control over the outcome.

The illusion of control can set us up for disappointment in both politics and personal relationships. In politics, believing we have more influence than we actually do can lead to flawed strategies that ignore the complexities of voter behavior and society. In relationships, thinking one person can single-handedly drive change or solve problems creates unnecessary pressure and frustration, as real progress often requires shared effort and individual choice.

Recognizing this cognitive bias helps us keep our expectations realistic, improving our decisions and interactions in both public and private life.

26. Self-Serving Bias

Self-serving bias is another mental shortcut that helps us protect our self-esteem. It's when we take credit for our successes but blame external factors for our failures. Let's explore how this bias shows up in politics and relationships.

In Politics

Election Wins and Losses

Winning feels great, and when a politician wins, they often credit their own skills and strategy. But when they lose, the blame shifts.

Winning: "I won because I'm a great leader with a brilliant campaign."
Losing: "I lost because the media was biased and the other party cheated."
Analysis: In this case, the politician is quick to praise their abilities for the victory but blames external forces for the defeat. This self-serving bias helps protect their ego, but it clouds reality—election results are shaped by more than just one person's actions. Voter behavior, party dynamics, and even external events play a huge role, whether they win or lose.

Policy Outcomes

Governments, too, like to take credit for success while pointing fingers when things go wrong.
Successful Policy: "Our economic policy worked because of our smart planning and execution."
Failed Policy: "The policy failed due to global economic issues and opposition from interest groups."
Analysis: Here, the government celebrates their success but blames failures on outside forces. While global trends and opposition do matter, ignoring mistakes or miscalculations in their planning can prevent them from learning and improving. Self-serving bias shields them from recognizing where they went wrong.

In Relationships

In relationships, self-serving bias can cause people to only see their role in the good times, while blaming the bad times on their partner.
Success: "My last relationship worked because I was loving and attentive."
Failure: "The breakup happened because my partner was emotionally unavailable."

Analysis: By only praising their own qualities and blaming their partner for failures, this person is missing the full picture. Relationships are complex, and both partners contribute to success or failure. Self-serving bias might protect their self-esteem, but it prevents them from reflecting on their own actions and growing from the experience.

Conflict Resolution

During a disagreement, one partner might believe they alone were responsible for solving the issue, while blaming their partner when things don't get better.

Resolved Conflict: "We fixed the issue because I stayed calm and communicated well."

Escalated Conflict: "The argument got worse because you were unreasonable and didn't listen."

Analysis: This mindset is self-serving bias in action. The person credits themselves for resolving the conflict but points fingers when things go wrong. In reality, conflicts are usually a two-way street, and resolving them requires effort from both people. This bias can block them from seeing their own role in the argument and recognizing that it takes both partners to make things right.

Self-serving bias allows us to keep a positive image of ourselves, but it can distort reality. In politics, it stops leaders from learning from their mistakes, which can lead to repeated failures. In relationships, it prevents individuals from reflecting on their own behavior and growing. Recognizing this bias helps us develop a more balanced view of our actions, leading to better decisions and healthier relationships.

27. Halo Effect

The halo effect is a cognitive bias where one positive trait or quality of a person or situation colors our entire perception of them, making everything about them seem better than it is. This can lead to overlooking flaws and making biased judgments. Let's explore some real-life examples in politics and relationships to see how the halo effect influences our thinking.

In Politics

Charismatic Leadership

Imagine a political leader who captivates the crowd with their charisma and powerful speeches.

Scenario: The leader is admired for their inspiring speeches and confident demeanor.

Argument: "Politician X is a great leader because they give inspiring speeches and always look confident."

Analysis: The halo effect takes hold when people equate the leader's charisma with their ability to govern. A talent for public speaking and exuding confidence is impressive, but it doesn't necessarily reflect decision-making skills, experience, or integrity. The halo effect can cloud voters' judgment, leading to support for leaders who may lack competence in areas critical for effective governance.

Reputation of a Political Party

Picture a political party that has a strong track record of economic success in the past.

Scenario: The party once boosted the economy by creating jobs and fostering growth.

Argument: "This party is the best for the economy because they've created jobs before."

Analysis: The halo effect here causes voters to associate the party's past success with its current ability, even when the party might be dealing with corruption, outdated policies, or poor leadership today. The glow of past accomplishments can overshadow current flaws, leading to decisions based more on history than on present reality.

In Relationships

Think of a situation where one partner is incredibly attractive, and this shapes how the other partner views them as a person.

Scenario: The partner's physical appearance influences how they're perceived overall.

Argument: "They must be a wonderful person because they're so good-looking."

Analysis: The halo effect occurs when physical attractiveness leads someone to assume the person also has other desirable traits like kindness, intelligence, or responsibility—without any real evidence. This can create unrealistic expectations, making the attractive partner seem perfect. But over time, these assumptions may lead to disappointment if they don't meet the idealized image.

A Single Act of Kindness

Now, imagine one partner doing something thoughtful, like organizing an elaborate surprise for their significant other.

Scenario: The partner plans a surprise birthday party that deeply touches the other.

Argument: "They're such a caring person because they planned this amazing surprise for me."

Analysis: While the surprise is a kind gesture, the halo effect might cause the recipient to overlook other issues in the relationship, like poor communication or lack of emotional support. One standout action shouldn't define a person's entire character, but the halo effect can skew perception, making it easier to ignore flaws because of one shining moment.

The halo effect can greatly influence how we perceive people and situations, impacting decisions in both politics and relationships. In politics, we may overestimate a leader's abilities or support a party based on past success, while ignoring current shortcomings. In relationships, we may idealize a partner based on one positive trait, leading to unrealistic expectations and a distorted view of who they truly are.

By being aware of the halo effect, we can avoid letting one quality overshadow everything else, leading to more balanced and informed decisions in both our public and personal lives.

28. False Consensus Effect

The false consensus effect is a fascinating psychological bias where people overestimate how much others share their beliefs, opinions, or behaviors. It can create misunderstandings, bad decisions, and unnecessary conflict because we assume others think like we do. Let's explore how this plays out in politics and relationships.

In Politics

Imagine a politician who strongly supports a controversial policy and believes the public is fully behind them.

Scenario: This politician is pushing for strict immigration laws, convinced the majority agrees with their stance.

Argument: "Most people want strict immigration controls because it's just common sense."

Analysis: The politician is falling into the trap of the false consensus effect. They assume their views are widely shared when, in reality, the issue might be far more divisive. By overestimating public agreement, they risk alienating voters who feel differently and may misread what the electorate actually wants. This can lead to ineffective policies and failed campaigns.

Political Campaign Strategies

Now, consider a candidate who builds their entire campaign around the issues they personally care about, assuming everyone else does too.

Scenario: The candidate focuses heavily on lowering taxes because they believe it's the top concern for all voters.

Argument: "Everyone cares most about lowering taxes, so that's what our campaign should focus on."

Analysis: The candidate is projecting their own priorities onto the public, missing out on other key voter concerns like healthcare or climate change. The false consensus effect blinds them to the diverse opinions of the electorate, which weakens their campaign strategy and might cost them crucial support from undecided voters.

In Relationships

Imagine one partner who loves going to the movies and assumes the other feels exactly the same.

Scenario: Every weekend, one partner plans a movie night, assuming it's what both of them enjoy most.

Argument: "We both love going to the movies every weekend because that's what everyone likes to do."

Analysis: The false consensus effect is at work here. One partner assumes their enthusiasm for movies is shared, but the other might secretly prefer a quiet evening at home or a different activity. If this assumption is never questioned, it can build up frustration, with one partner feeling their own interests are being ignored.

Communication Styles

Consider a couple where one partner believes in resolving conflicts immediately, assuming the other feels the same way.

Scenario: During disagreements, one partner insists on talking things out right away, convinced it's the best approach. **Argument:** "We both prefer to talk things out right away because that's the best way to solve problems." **Analysis:** Here, the false consensus effect leads one partner to believe their way of handling conflict is universally preferred. But the other might need time to cool off or think before engaging in a conversation. This difference in communication styles can cause tension if the assumption isn't addressed, with one partner feeling pressured and the other feeling unheard.

The false consensus effect can distort our view of reality in both politics and relationships. In politics, it can lead to misguided strategies and policies by assuming that one's views are universally accepted, while in relationships, it can cause misunderstandings and unmet expectations when partners assume they're on the same page without really checking. By recognizing this bias, we can open ourselves to more diverse perspectives, leading to better communication, improved decisions, and stronger connections in both public and personal life.

29. Sunk Cost Fallacy

The sunk cost fallacy is when we continue a behavior or endeavor because of previously invested resources (time, money, effort) rather than the current benefits or future potential. In other words, we hold on to something, not because it's good for us, but because we've already put in so much.

Imagine you're halfway through a movie. It's terrible—boring plot, wooden acting, and you're not enjoying it one bit. But you think, "I've already watched an hour; I might as well finish it." That thought, that feeling of needing to finish because of what you've already invested, is a classic example of the sunk cost fallacy.

Let's take a look at how the sunk cost fallacy sneaks into different areas of life, and why it's so important to recognize and avoid.

In Self-Help

Think of someone trying to stick to a diet. They've already bought a year's worth of meal plans and expensive supplements, but after a few months, it's clear the diet isn't working for them. They're constantly tired, stressed, and unhappy. However, instead of switching to something more suitable, they keep at it, thinking, "I've already spent so much on this; I can't just give up now."

The fallacy here is believing that past effort means you should keep going, even when it's no longer serving you. In self-help and personal development, this mindset can be dangerous. Holding onto old methods or strategies just because of the investment stops you from finding what truly works.

In contrast, those who are willing to let go of what's not serving them—whether it's a failed diet, bad habits, or a flawed approach to a goal—are free to explore better solutions. And that's where growth happens.

In Politics

Now let's turn to politics. Imagine a government has spent billions on a project—perhaps a large infrastructure plan. Halfway through, they realize it's not working. The public isn't benefiting, and costs are skyrocketing. But instead of scrapping the project, the leaders think, "We've already spent so much; stopping now would be a waste!"

This is the sunk cost fallacy at its worst. Politicians often continue with failed projects or policies to avoid looking like they've wasted money. But in reality, the money is already spent—continuing just digs the hole deeper.

Smart leaders know when to cut their losses. They realize that sticking to a bad decision doesn't redeem the wasted time or resources—it only multiplies the losses.

In Organizations

In businesses and organizations, the sunk cost fallacy can lead to massive inefficiencies. Let's say a company invests in a software upgrade. The team has poured months of work into it, but it's clear that the new system is causing more problems than it's solving. However, instead of switching to a better solution, the company decides to push forward. The reason? "We've already invested too much in this!"

This decision could lead to loss of productivity, frustrated employees, and eventually, lost profits. Recognizing when a strategy or investment isn't working and having the courage to pivot is essential for organizational success.

Some of the most successful companies know this. They cut projects that aren't working, no matter how much has been spent, and reallocate resources to what will move them forward. It's not about what's already been done—it's about what will work going forward.

In Relationships

Finally, let's talk about relationships—romantic, friendships, or even family ties. Picture this: You've been in a relationship for years, and things haven't been good for a while. There's arguing, dissatisfaction, or worse, emotional neglect. But you

stay. Why? "We've been together so long. I can't throw away all those years!"
This is the sunk cost fallacy in one of its most heartbreaking forms. Staying in a relationship out of a sense of obligation, simply because of the time you've already invested, often leads to prolonged pain and unhappiness.

Healthy relationships grow and adapt, and sometimes the best thing you can do is recognize when it's time to walk away. Letting go of what's no longer working makes room for healthier, more fulfilling connections.
The sunk cost fallacy is a powerful illusion. It makes us believe that we must continue with something just because we've already started. But clinging to past investments only weighs us down. The real power lies in recognizing when to let go, learn from the experience, and move forward—free from the burden of sunk costs.

So next time you find yourself stuck in a bad movie, bad job, or bad relationship, remember: it's okay to walk out. The price of holding on is often far greater than the cost of letting go.

30. The Forer Effect

Imagine you walk into a fortune teller's booth. She gazes into your eyes and says, "You have a great need for others to like and admire you, but you can be critical of yourself. You have some weaknesses, but you're generally able to compensate for them. There are times when you doubt whether you made the right decision."

What just happened is a classic example of the Forer Effect, a psychological phenomenon that makes people believe that vague, general statements are personal and specific to them. The Forer Effect is named after psychologist Bertram Forer, who in 1948 gave his students a personality test, then handed out a supposed personalized evaluation. In reality, everyone got the same list of general statements. Yet, most of them rated the accuracy of their description as high—thinking it was tailored just for them.

In Everyday Life

The Forer Effect is everywhere, from horoscopes to personality tests, and even in the advice we get from self-help books. It plays on our natural desire to find meaning and connection, and that's why understanding it is so important. Let's explore how the Forer Effect works in different areas of life, and why it matters.

In Self-Help

Let's start with self-help books and seminars. Imagine you pick up a bestselling self-help book, and within the first chapter, it tells you something like, "You're a person who's had struggles in the past, but you're determined to overcome them. You have hidden potential that's waiting to be unlocked."
This kind of statement feels powerful because it seems like it's speaking directly to your experience. The Forer Effect explains why this happens. The words are vague enough to apply to almost anyone, yet they feel personalized because we want to believe they reflect our unique situation.

In self-help, the Forer Effect can be both helpful and harmful. It can give us a sense of hope and motivation, but it can also lead us to overvalue generic advice or solutions that don't truly address our personal challenges. Being aware of the Forer

Effect helps us differentiate between truly useful insights and feel-good but overly broad statements.

In Cold Reading

Have you ever wondered how fortune tellers, psychics, or even media seem to know so much about people they've just met? Much of their success comes from the Forer Effect combined with a technique known as cold reading.

Cold reading is when a person, like a psychic, makes high-probability guesses and general statements that are likely to apply to many people. For example, a psychic might say, "You've experienced a recent loss, haven't you?" or "There's someone with the letter 'M' in your life who has been important to you." Many people will have some connection to a loss or know someone with that letter, and so the psychic's statement feels personal.

This trick works because of the Forer Effect. We naturally focus on the parts of a statement that resonate with us and ignore the parts that don't. A vague statement feels true because we fill in the details ourselves.

While cold reading can be entertaining, it's important to be aware of the Forer Effect in these situations. It helps us understand how psychics and fortune tellers operate and prevents us from being misled by what appears to be supernatural insight.

31 .The Reverse Halo Effect

Imagine meeting someone who makes a bad first impression. Maybe they're late to an appointment or say something a little rude. Now, without realizing it, you start seeing everything about them in a negative light. This is the reverse halo effect—where one negative trait overshadows everything else about a person, making even their good qualities seem worse than they really are.

It's like putting on a pair of glasses that tint everything in a dark, unflattering shade. Once you spot that one flaw, it becomes hard to see anything else, and it begins to cloud your judgment. Let's explore how this plays out in everyday life and how it affects our decisions and relationships.

Reverse Halo Effect & Our Decisions

The reverse halo effect can sneak up on us in subtle ways, shaping our choices without us even realizing it.

The Job Interview

Picture yourself as a hiring manager, interviewing a candidate. The person walks in, trips on the doorway, and nervously fumbles through the first few minutes of conversation. Instantly, you label them as clumsy and unprepared. Even though they might go on to give great answers and have an impressive resume, your mind is stuck on that bad start. Instead of seeing their potential, you only see the flaw. This can lead to dismissing someone who might actually be a great fit, simply because of one small misstep.

The Restaurant Experience

Or imagine going to a new restaurant, excited to try it out. As you sit down, the waiter spills a bit of water on the table. Annoying, right? Even though the food might be delicious and the atmosphere lovely, that one mistake keeps gnawing at you. You leave the restaurant thinking, "It wasn't that great." The waiter's tiny slip overshadowed everything else, affecting your entire experience.

In Relationships

In relationships, the reverse halo effect can be even more powerful and damaging. A single flaw or mistake can make it hard to see the good in someone, leading to misunderstandings, frustrations, and sometimes even the end of a relationship.

The Flawed First Impression

Let's say you go on a date. Your date shows up wearing something you find a bit off—maybe it's a shirt that doesn't quite match or shoes that seem outdated. Immediately, you start to judge their whole personality based on that one superficial detail. You might even begin to assume they're sloppy or out of touch, even though, deep down, you know clothing doesn't define a person. But that one detail clouds your view of everything else about them.

In Long-Term Relationships

In a long-term relationship, the reverse halo effect can creep in after a fight or disagreement. Imagine your partner forgets an important anniversary. You're hurt and disappointed, and suddenly, that one mistake makes you start questioning everything. "They never really pay attention," you think. "They're always so careless." Even if they've been thoughtful and loving most of the time, that one flaw makes it hard to see their good qualities anymore. It turns into a snowball effect, where every little thing they do starts to annoy you.

How It Can Break Down Trust

The reverse halo effect can also break down trust in a relationship. Maybe your partner tells a small lie about something insignificant, like forgetting to pick up groceries. That lie, though small, can make you question everything they say. Suddenly, you find yourself doubting them even when they're telling the truth. One flaw has made you see everything through a lens of suspicion.

The Lasting Impact

The reverse halo effect can have a lasting impact on relationships, both personal and professional. By focusing too much on someone's flaws, we risk missing out on deeper connections or opportunities. In romantic relationships, it can create unnecessary tension, making it hard to move past minor mistakes. At work, it can lead to unfair judgments and missed chances to see someone's true talents.

It's easy to fall into the trap of letting one flaw overshadow everything else, but being aware of the reverse halo effect can help us step back and take a more balanced view of the people around us.

Seeing Beyond the Flaws

The reverse halo effect teaches us an important lesson no one is perfect, and everyone has flaws. But when we let one mistake or trait define how we see someone, we do them—and ourselves—a disservice. Whether it's in relationships, at work, or even at a restaurant, it's worth remembering that one bad moment doesn't have to spoil everything. By looking beyond the flaws, we give ourselves a chance to see the bigger picture—and maybe even discover something wonderful that we almost missed.

32. Feigning Ignorance

Imagine you've just confronted someone about a serious issue. Maybe it's about a hurtful comment they made, or perhaps you've caught them in a lie. Instead of addressing the matter directly, they look at you with wide eyes, pretending not to understand. "What do you mean?" they ask, acting as if they have no idea what you're talking about. This is feigning ignorance, one of the most subtle yet powerful manipulation tactics used in personal relationships, politics, and beyond.

Feigning ignorance is when someone pretends not to know or understand something in order to avoid responsibility, deflect blame, or buy themselves time. It's a clever way of sidestepping an issue while making the other person feel either confused or overly aggressive for continuing to push the topic. The beauty of this tactic lies in its simplicity—by acting clueless, manipulators can shift the emotional burden back onto the person confronting them.

In Personal Relationships

Feigning ignorance is common in romantic and family relationships, often used as a defense mechanism when someone doesn't want to admit fault or confront uncomfortable truths. Take the example of a couple where one partner suspects the other of cheating. When confronted, the accused partner may respond with something like, "I don't know what you're talking about," or "What? Me? Why would you even think that?" By acting shocked and innocent, they deflect the accusation and force their partner to question their own judgment.

Consider a parent-child dynamic. A teenager sneaks out late at night, but when the parent confronts them, the teen might respond, "What do you mean? I didn't know we had a curfew!" Here, the teen is pretending not to understand the rules in order to avoid punishment. The parent, now unsure whether their child is truly oblivious or being deceptive, may let the issue slide, just to avoid further conflict.

In Politics

Feigning ignorance is a favorite tactic among politicians as well. When questioned about controversial policies or caught in a scandal, politicians often feign ignorance to dodge accountability. A classic example might be a government official claiming, "I wasn't aware of the details of the program," when accused of mishandling funds or making poor decisions.

Consider the Watergate scandal, where U.S. President Richard Nixon's administration was implicated in a massive cover-up. Many of the key figures involved initially claimed ignorance, stating they were unaware of the break-in or subsequent illegal activities. By playing dumb, they attempted to distance themselves from the wrongdoing, hoping to escape punishment or delay the investigation long enough for public interest to fade.

Another example lies in how politicians handle controversial global issues. During hearings or public addresses, they might feign ignorance about critical details in order to avoid taking a firm stance or accepting responsibility for unpopular decisions. This can be seen when leaders deflect difficult questions with vague responses like, "I need to look into that further," or, "I wasn't briefed on that specific matter," even if they were fully aware.

Why Feigning Ignorance Works

Feigning ignorance works because it exploits a fundamental aspect of human communication: most people don't want to come across as overly aggressive or accusatory. When someone pretends they don't understand what they've done wrong, it places the accuser in a tricky position. Should they push harder and risk appearing unreasonable? Or should they back off, feeling unsure whether the person is genuinely innocent?

This tactic also buys the manipulator time. In personal relationships, it can delay a confrontation, giving them space to craft a better defense. In politics, it can stall investigations or allow the individual to control the narrative. Feigning ignorance shifts the focus from the accused to the accuser, forcing them to prove the other person's wrongdoing rather than focusing on the issue at hand.

Breaking the Cycle

The best way to counter this tactic is persistence and clarity. If you suspect someone is feigning ignorance, stay calm but firm. Repeat the facts, ask direct questions, and refuse to be sidetracked by their act of confusion. In relationships, establishing clear boundaries and expectations can prevent people from relying on this manipulation technique. In politics, demanding transparency and holding leaders accountable for their actions, even when they play dumb, can help maintain integrity in governance.

Feigning ignorance may seem like a harmless act, but it can deeply undermine trust in personal and professional relationships alike. Recognizing this tactic for what it is allows you to see through the smokescreen and address the real issue at hand. After all, pretending not to know doesn't erase the truth—it only delays it.

33. Appeal to Motive

Imagine this: You confront someone about a decision they made or an action they took. Instead of addressing the facts of the matter, they dismiss your concerns by questioning your motives. "You're only saying that because you're jealous," they might say. Or, "You just want to undermine my success." This is an example of the Appeal to Motive manipulation tactic—a subtle, psychological way to divert attention from the issue at hand by casting doubt on the accuser's intentions.

The Appeal to Motive fallacy occurs when someone dismisses an argument or criticism not by addressing its validity but by attacking the supposed underlying motives of the person making the argument. The tactic distracts from the actual substance of the conversation and instead focuses on the presumed intentions behind the critique.

In both personal relationships and politics, this tactic is used to avoid accountability and shift the conversation in a different direction, making it difficult to address the real issue.

In Personal Relationships

Appeal to Motive is a common tactic in relationships, especially when there's conflict or tension. For example, imagine a couple where one partner brings up concerns about the other's excessive spending. Instead of discussing the financial issue, the partner might respond with, "You're only saying that because you want to control me," or "You're just upset because you can't buy what you want." By questioning the motives, the accused shifts the conversation from the issue (the spending) to an emotional one, where the focus is now on the accuser's alleged jealousy or need for control.

Another example could be between friends. Let's say one friend criticizes the other for frequently canceling plans. Instead of addressing the habit of flaking out, the accused might say, "You just don't want me to have other friends," flipping the focus back on the accuser's insecurities rather than their own behavior.

In Politics

Appeal to Motive is a go-to strategy in political debates and campaigns. When politicians are confronted with criticism about policies or decisions, they often respond by questioning the motives of their critics rather than addressing the substance of the critique. A classic example might be when a government is criticized for a controversial policy. Instead of defending the policy on its merits, a politician might say, "The opposition is only against this because they want to make us look bad," or, "They're just playing politics to win votes." In this way, the critic's argument is dismissed without ever being addressed.

Consider the use of this tactic in environmental debates. If a political leader opposes new regulations to curb pollution, environmental advocates might criticize them for ignoring scientific evidence. In response, the politician could say, "They're just trying to scare people to push their agenda," deflecting the conversation away from the science and toward an accusation about the advocates' motives.

Why Appeal to Motive Works

Appeal to Motive works because it plays on emotions rather than logic. By questioning someone's motives, the accused puts the accuser on the defensive, forcing them to prove their intentions rather than focusing on the actual issue. It also muddies the waters, making it harder for others involved in the conversation to stay focused on the facts.

This tactic is especially powerful in personal relationships, where emotions run high, and in politics, where the stakes are often about public perception and influence.

Breaking the Cycle

The key to dealing with the Appeal to Motive fallacy is to stay focused on the facts. When someone questions your motives, calmly redirect the conversation back to the issue at hand. In personal relationships, it helps to separate emotions from the argument by saying something like, "My feelings aren't the issue here. Let's talk about what we're actually discussing." In political debates, keeping the focus on evidence, data, and logical reasoning can help break through the deflection.

The Appeal to Motive tactic is a subtle yet powerful way people deflect from being held accountable, both in relationships and in politics. By questioning the intentions of others, manipulators shift the focus away from the real issue and put the accuser on the defensive. Recognizing this tactic is the first step to overcoming it. By staying focused on facts and pushing back against emotional deflection, we can prevent manipulators from steering conversations away from what's important.

34. Intentionally Convoluted Explanations

Have you ever asked someone a simple question, only to be met with an explanation so complicated and confusing that you ended up more puzzled than before? If so, you may have encountered the manipulation tactic known as intentionally convoluted explanation. This tactic involves using unnecessarily complex language, vague details, and roundabout reasoning to confuse, mislead, or deflect from the real issue. It's a way of hiding the truth in plain sight by wrapping it in layers of unnecessary complexity.

Let's explore how this manipulation works in both personal relationships and politics, with real-world examples that show just how powerful—and frustrating—this tactic can be.

In Personal Relationships

Imagine a situation where a partner suspects their significant other of lying about where they were the night before. Instead of giving a straightforward answer like, "I was at work," the person being questioned might say something like, "Well, after my meeting ran longer than expected due to unforeseen circumstances, I had to consult with my colleague about this upcoming project which, by the way, required a whole new set of deliverables..."

By the end of this winding explanation, the original question has been lost, and the partner is left more confused than ever. This convoluted response can be a deliberate attempt to evade the truth without directly lying. The idea is that the more complicated the explanation, the harder it becomes to scrutinize.

This tactic is particularly effective because the person on the receiving end may feel too overwhelmed to ask more questions. They may even start to doubt their own instincts, thinking, "Maybe it's just me—I don't understand because I'm not familiar with the details."

In Politics

In the world of politics, intentionally convoluted explanations are a favorite tool for avoiding accountability. When politicians are questioned about controversial decisions or policies, they often respond with highly technical jargon, vague references, or long-winded answers that are difficult to follow.

Take, for example, a political leader being asked why government funds were used inefficiently on a project. Instead of saying, "We mismanaged the funds," they might respond with something like, "The allocation of resources had to undergo a multifaceted reevaluation based on both external and internal economic metrics, which led to a shift in the execution phase due to unforeseen budgetary realignments…"

The listener is left unsure of what just happened and may hesitate to press further, assuming that the issue is too complex to understand. By using convoluted language, the politician successfully dodges the question and avoids taking responsibility.

Real-World Examples

In the business world, intentionally convoluted explanations are often used by companies to downplay problems or mistakes. Let's say a company is questioned about a faulty product that's been causing issues for customers. Instead of admitting fault, a spokesperson might say, "The operational inefficiencies in our supply chain, combined with the unpredictable variables in our production environment, resulted in a temporary divergence from the optimal product quality benchmarks we usually maintain."

What does that even mean? The customer is left bewildered, with no clear answer, and the company gets to avoid direct blame. This kind of jargon-filled response serves to mask the problem and make it seem like it's too complicated for the average person to grasp.

A Tool in the Hands of Religious Figures

Intentionally convoluted explanations aren't only the realm of politics or business—they're often used by religious figures as well. This technique can be particularly powerful when employed in the context of faith, as many followers look up to religious leaders as figures of authority, trusting them to have the answers to complex, existential questions. When these leaders intentionally complicate their explanations, they obscure the truth, deflect difficult questions, and reinforce their authority over their followers.

How It Works in Religion

In religious contexts, intentionally convoluted explanations are often used to keep followers from questioning too much or to maintain a sense of mystery around doctrines that may be controversial, unclear, or even nonsensical. By using theological jargon, abstract ideas, and lengthy scripture references, religious figures can effectively sidestep difficult questions or doubts that arise from their congregation.

Ex: The "Problem of Evil"

Consider a follower who asks a religious leader a tough question: "If God is all-good and all-powerful, why does evil exist?" This is a classic philosophical and theological problem, often called the Problem of Evil. Instead of providing a clear and direct response, a religious figure might reply with something like:

"Ah, my child, the nature of good and evil is far more complex than the human mind can fully comprehend. The divine will operates on a plane that transcends our earthly understanding, wherein God's wisdom aligns all things for the ultimate purpose, far beyond what we see as immediate pain or suffering. Evil, as perceived in the temporal world, could merely be a fragment of a larger divine plan, one that brings all creation to ultimate redemption."

This long, convoluted response leaves the follower in awe of the complexity but without a clear answer. They may feel more confused, but at the same time, they are more likely to accept the answer because they believe they lack the spiritual knowledge to fully grasp it.

Ex: Financial Contributions

Let's take another example involving financial contributions in a religious organization. If a congregation member questions why so much money is being funneled into a lavish project, rather than being used for charitable work, the leader might use convoluted explanations to deflect:

"You see, the spiritual and material aspects of our community must be balanced in such a way that they reflect the glory of our divine mission. The allocation of resources is a deeply considered process, rooted in sacred traditions that ensure the sustainability of our spiritual infrastructure, which in turn enables us to extend our reach and impact, far beyond immediate humanitarian concerns..."

By the end of this explanation, the original question—about why the funds aren't being used for charity—is buried under a thick layer of abstract concepts. The follower may be too overwhelmed or confused to challenge it further.

Why It Works in Religion

This tactic works particularly well in religious settings for a few reasons:

Reverence for Authority:

Followers often see religious leaders as wise and divinely inspired, so they're less likely to challenge them.

The Mystique of Faith:

Religion often deals with mysteries of the universe, life, and death. Followers are conditioned to accept that some things are beyond their understanding.

Fear of Blasphemy:

In many religious settings, questioning a leader's explanation could be seen as a lack of faith, or worse, as blasphemy. This discourages further scrutiny.

Intentionally convoluted explanations can serve as a manipulative tool in religious contexts, leaving followers confused but obedient. By cloaking simple truths in complexity, religious figures can avoid difficult questions, reinforce their authority, and maintain control over their congregation. Whether it's explaining the existence of evil or justifying financial practices, this manipulation tactic relies on the follower's reverence and fear of questioning their faith.

It's important to recognize this tactic when it's being used, whether in religion, politics, or personal relationships, and to ask for clarity in the face of confusing or evasive explanations.

How to Spot and Disarm

The key to breaking through an intentionally convoluted explanation is to ask direct, specific questions. If someone gives you a complex answer, follow up with something like, "Can you explain that in simpler terms?" or "What exactly does that mean?" Keep the focus on getting clear, concise information.

In politics, this can mean holding leaders accountable by demanding straightforward answers in debates or public forums. In personal relationships, it means not letting someone dodge a question by burying it in layers of confusion.

35. Love Bombing

Love bombing is a powerful manipulation tactic where someone overwhelms you with excessive attention, affection, and gifts to gain control over your emotions. At first glance, it feels like a dream—who wouldn't want to be showered with love? But beneath the surface, love bombing is a tool used by manipulators to create emotional dependency, and once that's established, the darker motives are revealed.

Personal Relationships

In personal relationships, love bombing can look like a whirlwind romance where the person seems too good to be true. They might shower you with praise, tell you they love you within a few days of meeting, and constantly want to be around you. While it can feel exhilarating, this fast-tracked affection is not a sign of genuine connection but a strategy to make you emotionally dependent on them.

For instance, Emily met Jake, who seemed perfect. Within a week, he was sending her flowers every day, texting her constantly, and talking about their future together. She was swept off her feet. But slowly, Jake's behavior changed. He began isolating her from friends and family, demanding her attention, and using the love he initially showed to guilt-trip her whenever she didn't meet his expectations. The intense affection quickly morphed into control, leaving Emily emotionally trapped.

In Politics

Love bombing isn't just for romantic relationships; it's also a common tactic in politics. Politicians sometimes use this tactic during campaigns, presenting themselves as saviors who will fix all of a country's problems. They flatter the electorate, making grand promises and showering communities with attention during election periods. But once they've won the votes, the overwhelming affection stops, and often, so do the promises.

For example, a politician running for office might make frequent visits to a neglected area, promising resources, jobs, and infrastructure improvements. During their campaign, they attend every local event, offer financial support, and praise the community's resilience. The community feels seen and heard, giving their votes in exchange for hope. But after the election, those visits and promises often disappear, leaving the people feeling abandoned. The love was just a tool for power.

In Religion

In religious settings, love bombing can be used to recruit new members into cult-like groups or high-control environments. A new recruit might be showered with acceptance, a sense of belonging, and constant affirmations of love and purpose. This strategy is designed to make them feel special, wanted, and secure in the group's embrace. But once they're in deep, that same group may begin to control their actions, thoughts, and associations, using the initial love as a tool for manipulation.

For example, a person may join a religious group where everyone is overly friendly and welcoming, making them feel like they've found a spiritual family. They might be invited to countless group activities, where they are celebrated and given attention. But once they commit, the group starts demanding loyalty, financial contributions, or even cutting off ties with "outsiders." The initial affection was not unconditional love—it was a bait to gain control.

Why Love Bombing Works

Love bombing is effective because it plays on a basic human need for connection, validation, and love. We all want to feel valued and special, and when someone offers us that, it's easy to lower our defenses. By flooding the target with affection, the manipulator creates an emotional bond quickly. Once the target is hooked, the love and attention become a currency for control. The fear of losing that affection often leads to compliance.

Love bombing is a seductive yet dangerous manipulation tactic used to build emotional dependency in personal relationships, politics, and even religion. While it may start with overwhelming love and attention, it often ends in control and emotional entrapment. By recognizing the signs and understanding the tactics, individuals can safeguard themselves from falling into the sweet trap of manipulative love.

36. Fear-Mongering

Personal Relationships

In personal relationships, fear-mongering often surfaces as a way to control or manipulate a partner. Imagine a toxic relationship where one partner constantly warns the other that leaving them would lead to disaster. "If you leave me, you'll never find anyone else," or "Without me, your life will fall apart," are common phrases that evoke fear and insecurity. The manipulator creates a narrative where they are the only source of safety, and everything outside the relationship is dangerous.

Take the case of Sarah, whose boyfriend, Matt, often told her that the world was filled with people waiting to hurt her. He insisted that she needed him to navigate through life safely, even though he was the one isolating her from friends and family. By painting a world filled with threats, Matt kept Sarah dependent on him, paralyzed by fear of the unknown.

Fear-Mongering in Politics

Politicians have long mastered the use of fear-mongering to control public opinion and gain support. In many elections, fear becomes a central theme. The tactic works by focusing on potential dangers—real or imagined—that make people feel anxious or threatened. By offering themselves as the only solution to those dangers, politicians manipulate voters into siding with them.

One clear example is the frequent use of fear-based rhetoric during election campaigns. A candidate might warn that if their opponent wins, it will lead to economic collapse, widespread crime, or even war. By focusing on negative consequences and heightening the sense of fear, they steer voters away from rational decision-making and toward emotionally driven choices. In the U.S., fear of immigration has been used as a political weapon, with politicians portraying immigrants as dangerous criminals, even when data suggests otherwise.

Fear-Mongering in Religion

Religious institutions, both historical and modern, often use fear-mongering to keep followers in line. By threatening eternal damnation or punishment in the afterlife, religious leaders can ensure obedience. The fear of divine retribution can be a strong motivator, making individuals comply with religious rules out of fear of punishment rather than genuine belief.

Why Fear-Mongering Works

Fear is deeply ingrained in human psychology as a survival mechanism. When we feel threatened, our brains go into a fight-or-flight mode, focusing on the danger at hand and trying to avoid it at all costs. Manipulators take advantage of this instinct. By exaggerating threats or creating fictional dangers, they distract people from logical thinking and push them into emotional decisions.

When people are scared, they often look for someone to trust—someone who promises to save them from whatever they're afraid of. This is where the manipulator steps in.

Whether it's a partner in a relationship, a politician offering solutions to a fabricated crisis, or a religious leader warning of eternal damnation, fear-mongering works because it taps into one of our most primal emotions.

Fear-mongering is a dangerous manipulation tactic that thrives in personal relationships, politics, and religion. By using fear to control emotions and decisions, manipulators can push people into actions they wouldn't take under normal circumstances. Recognizing and challenging fear-based rhetoric is crucial for breaking free from this form of control and making decisions based on facts, not fear.

37. Appeal to Popularity (Bandwagon Effect)

The appeal to popularity, also known as the "bandwagon effect," is a powerful manipulation tactic that plays on the human desire to belong. This technique pushes people to accept a belief, idea, or course of action simply because "everyone else is doing it." It thrives on the assumption that the majority can't be wrong, and it's often used in personal relationships, politics, and religion to sway decisions and shape behavior.

Personal Relationships

In personal relationships, the bandwagon effect can show up when someone feels pressured to conform to a group's opinions or actions. Imagine a friend group where most people are on board with a particular decision, such as planning a vacation or agreeing on an activity. Even if one person disagrees, they might suppress their opinion to fit in, not wanting to be seen as the odd one out.

Take, for instance, the story of Emily. She didn't like the idea of going on a trip to a destination her friends chose, but since everyone else was excited and planning, she felt the pressure to go along. She didn't want to be labeled as difficult or feel left out, so she jumped on the bandwagon and participated, even though it wasn't what she wanted.
This tactic can be harmful when people set aside their own desires, values, or beliefs to follow the crowd, losing their individuality in the process.

In Politics

The bandwagon effect is a staple in politics, especially during election campaigns. Politicians and their teams often use this tactic to create the illusion of widespread support for their candidate or cause. When people see large crowds at rallies, hear polling numbers that favor one side, or see their neighbors endorsing a certain candidate, they may start to question their own stance, feeling compelled to support what seems like the "winning side."

For example, during election season, voters might hear statements like, "Everyone is voting for this candidate, don't be left out!" Such messaging makes it seem as though a majority is already on board, nudging undecided or wavering individuals to follow suit. In reality, the claim of universal support may be exaggerated or untrue, but the emotional pull of wanting to belong to the majority group is strong enough to sway many voters.

This bandwagon effect can also affect political opinion polls. When a candidate is leading in the polls, more people may be inclined to vote for them simply because they don't want to back a "losing" candidate, reinforcing the popularity of the frontrunner without deeper scrutiny.

In Religion

Religion, too, has long been a fertile ground for the bandwagon effect. In many religious groups, especially tightly-knit communities or large gatherings, there's a sense of safety in numbers. When everyone around you shares the same faith, beliefs, and practices, it's easy to assume that those beliefs must be correct. After all, can so many people really be wrong?

Take, for example, the story of Ravi, who grew up in a deeply religious community where everyone around him practiced the same rituals and adhered to the same beliefs. Although Ravi privately questioned some of these teachings, the overwhelming consensus of his family and community made it difficult for him to express his doubts. The idea that everyone believed the same thing created an implicit pressure on him to conform, even though his inner thoughts were in conflict.

In some cases, the bandwagon effect in religion can be amplified through charismatic leaders or high-profile conversions. When celebrities or influential people publicly declare their faith, followers of that religion often use their popularity to encourage others to join, reinforcing the idea that it's a "right" or desirable belief because influential people endorse it.

Why the Bandwagon Effect Works

At its core, the bandwagon effect taps into the human need for belonging and acceptance. Humans are social creatures, and being part of a group feels reassuring. No one wants to be the outcast, so when faced with the choice of standing out or blending in, most people choose to follow the crowd, especially when the crowd seems overwhelmingly in favor of something.

The bandwagon effect also reduces the mental effort required to make decisions. Instead of analyzing the details, researching, or forming an independent opinion, people take a mental shortcut: "If everyone else thinks this is right, it must be right." It's a shortcut that helps people avoid the discomfort of making a possibly unpopular choice.

38. The Scapegoating

Scapegoating refers to singling out one person or group for blame, regardless of whether or not they are actually responsible. This tactic works because it's easier to blame one target than to face the complexity of a problem. Instead of confronting underlying issues, the scapegoat becomes a convenient "solution," bearing the emotional or literal consequences.

The term originates from ancient Jewish traditions where a goat, symbolically carrying the sins of the people, was sent into the wilderness. Today, that same idea lives on in how we shift blame onto others, allowing us to avoid accountability and responsibility.

Imagine a family of four, where one child is constantly blamed for everything that goes wrong—the lost keys, the broken vase, even the strained marriage of the parents. This child, feeling confused and unfairly treated, doesn't know why they are the target. This is scapegoating, an ancient and deeply ingrained manipulation tactic where one person or group is unfairly blamed for the problems of others.

This tactic has a long history. It not only appears in personal relationships but also plays a key role in politics and religion. Let's dive into how scapegoating works, why people use it, and some striking real-life examples.

Personal Relationships

In families or close relationships, scapegoating can be devastating. One member is often seen as the "problem child" or the "black sheep." This person becomes the target for frustrations, anxieties, and unresolved conflicts that are actually rooted elsewhere.

Ex: The Blamed Child

Consider a household where a father is struggling with work-related stress, and the mother feels emotionally distant. Instead of addressing their strained relationship, they constantly criticize their teenage son, accusing him of being lazy, rebellious, and the reason for the family tension. While the teenager may have his own challenges, he is unfairly burdened with the blame for the breakdown in the family dynamic.

The parents find temporary relief by focusing their frustration on him, but in reality, this tactic only deepens the real issues—eventually leading to resentment and emotional damage.

Politics

Political leaders and governments have long used scapegoating to unite their followers and divert attention from their own failings. When an issue arises—whether it's economic decline, job losses, or societal unrest—scapegoating provides an easy way out by blaming a specific group.

Ex: Immigrants as Scapegoats

A well-known example can be seen during economic recessions when immigrants are often blamed for job shortages. Politicians may claim that immigrants are "stealing jobs" or draining resources, even though many economic studies prove otherwise. This manipulates public opinion, making one group a convenient target, while diverting attention from more complex factors like economic policy, technological changes, or global markets.

By turning immigrants into scapegoats, leaders unite their base against a common "enemy," distracting from systemic issues that are harder to address. The scapegoated group bears the brunt of hostility, while the real problems remain unsolved.

Religion

Religion, too, is no stranger to scapegoating. Historically, religious leaders and communities have used scapegoating to explain hardship, misfortune, or moral failings, often attributing these to the actions of a specific group or individual.

Ex: Witch Hunts in History

One of the most haunting examples of religious scapegoating is the witch hunts in Europe and the American colonies during the 16th and 17th centuries. In times of famine, disease, or social turmoil, people were quick to accuse women—often those who were vulnerable or socially marginalized—of witchcraft. These women were blamed for everything from poor harvests to unexplained deaths, becoming the scapegoats for a community desperate for answers.

In reality, these accusations were rarely based on any factual evidence. They were often driven by fear, superstition, and a need for a simple solution to a complex issue. The witches, like all scapegoats, became the embodiment of the community's collective anxieties, unfairly suffering for the misfortunes of others.

Why Do We Scapegoating?

Scapegoating is, at its core, a defense mechanism. It's a way for individuals or groups to protect themselves from the painful truth. Whether it's a troubled marriage, a political failure, or a society dealing with uncertainty, the act of blaming someone else is a way to avoid the difficult process of self-reflection or systemic change.

39. Loaded Questions

Imagine sitting down with a friend who suddenly asks, "Why do you always ignore my messages?" Even though you might respond with confusion—because you haven't ignored them—you're already caught in a trap. This is a classic example of a loaded question.

A loaded question is a type of manipulation that sneaks an unfair assumption into a seemingly innocent query. The person being asked is set up to lose no matter how they answer. It's a subtle but powerful tactic, often used in personal relationships, politics, and even religious discussions, to corner someone or sway an audience. Let's explore what loaded questions are, how they work, and some interesting real-life examples of this sneaky strategy in action.

For example, imagine being asked, "Have you stopped lying to me?" This question assumes that you've been lying. Whether you answer "yes" or "no," you're trapped into admitting you were a liar at some point. The trick is subtle, but powerful.

Personal Relationships

In personal relationships, loaded questions can cause tension and create misunderstandings. They often appear during arguments or difficult conversations, where one person feels the need to gain control or shift blame.

Ex: The Accusatory Partner

Consider a couple, John and Sarah, who have been arguing more frequently. John asks, "Why don't you ever appreciate the things I do for you?" This question isn't just about John wanting an answer—it's loaded with the assumption that Sarah never appreciates him, putting her immediately on the defensive.

If Sarah tries to explain or defend herself, she's already playing into the idea that John's assumption is correct. Instead of having a calm discussion about how they both feel, Sarah is now scrambling to deny something that may not be true. The conversation becomes about whether she's ungrateful, rather than addressing the real issue—maybe they're both stressed, or they haven't communicated well lately.

In relationships, loaded questions are often used unconsciously, out of frustration or hurt. But they lead to misunderstandings, making productive conversations nearly impossible.

Politics

Politics is one of the most common arenas where loaded questions thrive. Politicians and media personalities often use these kinds of questions to put their opponents on the defensive, making it difficult to give a straightforward answer without looking bad.

Ex: The Political Debate Trap

Picture a heated political debate where a candidate is asked, "How long are you going to continue supporting policies that hurt working-class families?" The question assumes that the candidate's policies are already hurting working-class families. Even if the candidate doesn't believe that's true, answering the question directly makes it seem like they're admitting guilt or trying to justify harmful policies.

Instead of addressing the actual issues at hand, the candidate is stuck defending themselves from a false premise. This is a classic use of loaded questions in politics—they redirect the conversation, force the opponent into a corner, and make the person asking the question look like they're in control.

Loaded questions can also be used in interviews or press conferences to sway public opinion. For example, if a journalist asks a leader, "What do you plan to do about your administration's failure to prevent the housing crisis?" the leader must first address the assumption that their administration is responsible for the crisis, regardless of whether that's actually true.

Religion

In religious discussions, loaded questions can shape debates and silence opposition. These questions can be framed in such a way that the person answering seems to admit to a moral or spiritual failing, regardless of their actual beliefs.

Ex: Challenging Religious Beliefs

Consider someone questioning another's religious beliefs: "How can you claim to be a good person when you don't believe in God?" This is a loaded question that assumes being a good person is directly tied to belief in God. By answering, the person is forced to address the assumption, even though the original question was unfair and oversimplified.

In religious communities, loaded questions are sometimes used to reinforce group beliefs and make dissenting voices appear morally flawed. If someone tries to question or challenge a belief, they might be asked something like, "Why are you trying to cause division in the church?" This question suggests that questioning beliefs or practices is equivalent to causing harm, which makes it difficult for anyone to express doubts or concerns without looking like a troublemaker.

Why Do People Use Loaded Questions?

Loaded questions are a tool of manipulation because they're designed to put the other person on the defensive. They work because they blend two things: an innocent question and an underlying assumption. This gives the person asking the question a sense of control over the conversation, while making the person answering feel cornered or guilty.

In the end, breaking free from loaded questions isn't just about winning arguments. It's about creating space for genuine dialogue, where assumptions are laid bare, and everyone is given the chance to speak and be heard.

40. The Gish Gallop

Have you ever been in a conversation where the other person throws so many points at you—one after another—that you don't know where to start? By the time you try to address one, they've already jumped to another. This overwhelming flood of information is a manipulation tactic called the Gish Gallop.

Named after a controversial debater, Duane Gish, the Gish Gallop involves bombarding someone with a rapid-fire series of arguments, facts, or claims, often without giving them time to respond or check the accuracy. The goal isn't to have a meaningful conversation but to overwhelm and win through sheer volume. It's commonly used in personal relationships, political debates, and even religious discussions to gain an upper hand and avoid accountability. This tactic isn't about quality arguments but quantity. It's about winning by exhausting the other person's ability to respond.

Personal Relationships

In personal relationships, the Gish Gallop often shows up during arguments or conflicts, where one partner might use it to deflect responsibility or confuse the other person. Instead of staying on one topic and resolving it, the conversation gets flooded with unrelated issues, making it hard to address the real problem.

Ex: The Partner Who Changes the Subject

Let's say Emily confronts her partner, Jake, about forgetting their anniversary. Instead of owning up to the mistake, Jake responds with a flood of unrelated issues: "Oh, I forgot the anniversary? Well, last week you were late picking me up from work. And remember last month when you didn't do the dishes for three days? Plus, you never ask about my day anymore. And what about that time you ignored my texts last summer?"
Suddenly, the conversation has shifted from a single missed anniversary to a laundry list of grievances. Emily, overwhelmed, doesn't know which accusation to address first. This tactic leaves her on the defensive, unable to deal with the initial issue because Jake has overwhelmed her with multiple complaints.

In relationships, the Gish Gallop deflects responsibility, making it difficult to resolve conflicts. It's a way to avoid admitting fault by shifting the focus elsewhere—creating chaos where there should be clarity.

Politics

In politics, the Gish Gallop is a common debate tactic, especially in televised debates or interviews, where time is limited. Politicians use it to overwhelm their opponents or audiences with a flood of statements, making it impossible to fact-check or counter every point in real time. The sheer volume of claims makes the speaker seem knowledgeable and confident, even if many of their points are inaccurate.

Ex: The Political Debate Overload

Imagine a televised debate where one candidate, Alex, is asked about their environmental policy. Instead of giving a direct answer, Alex launches into a whirlwind of points: "Well, first, we need to talk about how the other candidate's economic policy will destroy jobs. And let's not forget the healthcare crisis. Plus, we're seeing a rise in crime rates. Also, what about education reform, which has been totally ignored?"

By the time Alex finishes, the audience—and the opponent—is overwhelmed. The original question about the environment has been buried under a pile of unrelated issues. The opponent now has too many points to address, making it difficult to respond meaningfully in the limited time. Even if Alex's statements are exaggerated or misleading, the tactic works because it floods the conversation with so much information that it's hard to debunk all of it.

The Gish Gallop in politics often leaves voters with an impression of authority and confidence, even when the arguments are flimsy or disconnected from the truth.

Religion

In religious debates or discussions, the Gish Gallop can be used to overwhelm those questioning or exploring their faith. Religious leaders or community members might use this tactic to bombard a skeptic or doubter with numerous theological points, moral arguments, or scripture quotes, making it difficult for the individual to keep up or respond thoughtfully.

Ex: The Overwhelming Religious Debate

Imagine a discussion between a skeptic and a deeply religious person about the existence of God. The skeptic asks one clear question: "How can a loving God allow so much suffering in the world?" Instead of addressing this difficult and complex question, the religious person responds with a flood of points:

"Well, first, you need to understand free will. Also, look at how much good religion has done for charity. Plus, the Bible explains suffering in the story of Job. And, by the way, science still can't explain the origins of life. And don't forget, prayer has been scientifically proven to help people feel better. Oh, and have you considered the moral collapse of society without religion?"

The skeptic is left spinning, trying to figure out which argument to address. The initial question about suffering is buried under a pile of unrelated points, leaving the skeptic feeling overwhelmed and unable to respond.

In religious contexts, the Gish Gallop can shut down meaningful discussions by overwhelming the other person with so many points that they can't engage with any of them fully.

Why Do People Use the Gish Gallop?

The Gish Gallop is effective because it creates confusion and overwhelms the person on the receiving end. It works on the principle that it's easier to throw out numerous claims than to refute them. Here's why people use this tactic:

Deflection: It shifts focus away from a single issue, allowing the person using the tactic to avoid accountability.
Appeal to authority: A barrage of information can make the speaker seem knowledgeable, even when their points are weak or irrelevant.
Time pressure: In debates or conversations with limited time, the Gish Gallop leaves the opponent with no chance to respond to every point.
Psychological overload: Flooding someone with multiple arguments overwhelms their mental capacity to process and refute each claim, leading to frustration or submission.

How to Defend it?

If you find yourself up against a Gish Gallop, the key is not to fall into the trap of addressing every point. Here are some strategies to protect yourself:
Stay focused: Don't get distracted by the flood of arguments. Identify the main issue and bring the conversation back to it. For example, if Jake throws a barrage of complaints at Emily, she might say, "We can talk about all these issues later, but right now, let's focus on why you forgot our anniversary."
Challenge the tactic: Call out the manipulation. In a debate or conversation, you can point out that the other person is throwing too many unrelated points into the mix and that it's not a fair way to have a discussion.
Take your time: Don't feel pressured to respond to every

single point immediately. In debates, you can often say, "Let's address one thing at a time."

Fact-check later: If someone uses a Gish Gallop in public, such as in politics, there's no need to debunk every point in real time. Take note of the claims and fact-check them afterward, highlighting the errors or exaggerations.

The Gish Gallop is a powerful tool in manipulation, used to overwhelm, confuse, and win arguments through sheer volume, rather than quality. Whether in personal relationships, politics, or religion, it can derail meaningful conversations and prevent real resolution.

41. Ingratiation

Ingratiation is the act of using compliments, flattery, or agreeableness to win someone's favor or approval. It's a form of subtle manipulation where the goal is to make the other person feel good about themselves, while the ingratiator gains influence or advantages in return.

Unlike more aggressive forms of manipulation, ingratiation is smooth and often goes unnoticed. The person being flattered may not even realize they're being influenced because everyone likes hearing good things about themselves. The danger of ingratiation lies in the fact that it's often insincere—people aren't being praised because they've earned it but because the ingratiator wants something from them.

Imagine a coworker who constantly showers their boss with compliments—about their leadership, their style, even how they make coffee. At first, it might seem harmless, even kind. But what if this endless praise had an ulterior motive? What if the compliments were designed not just to express admiration but to win favor, gain an advantage, or influence decisions? This is a classic example of ingratiation—a subtle manipulation tactic where someone uses flattery, charm, or overly helpful behavior to get what they want. It's a tool often seen in personal relationships, politics, and religious contexts, and while it can sometimes appear harmless, ingratiation can be a way to mask deeper, self-serving intentions.

Let's explore how ingratiation works, why it's so effective, and some real-life examples of how this tactic plays out in different areas of life.

Personal Relationships

In personal relationships, ingratiation can appear as excessive praise, over-the-top kindness, or being overly agreeable. While we all appreciate kindness, ingratiation can cross the line when it's used to manipulate someone into doing something they might not otherwise want to do.

Ex: The Friend Who Always Agrees

Take Mia and her friend Jess, for example. Jess is always showering Mia with compliments—how smart she is, how great her sense of style is, and how she always knows the best places to eat. At first, Mia feels flattered. But over time, she notices something: Jess always agrees with her, even when Mia is wrong. When Mia suggests things that Jess doesn't enjoy, like going to restaurants Jess doesn't like or watching movies she has no interest in, Jess still says, "Great idea! You're the best at picking things."

Why does Jess do this? It turns out, Jess is using ingratiation to avoid confrontation and keep Mia happy because she wants to stay on Mia's good side. Maybe Jess needs Mia's help or values her connections, but instead of being honest about her own feelings, she chooses to ingratiate herself by always praising Mia and agreeing with her. Over time, this creates an unbalanced friendship, where Mia may not even realize she's being manipulated.

Ingratiation in Politics

Politics is a stage where ingratiation thrives. Politicians often use flattery and praise to charm voters, influential leaders, or donors. It's not just about being likable—it's about winning favor that can translate into votes, financial support, or political alliances.

Ex: The Politician Who Flatters to Win

Imagine a politician giving a speech in a small town during election season. They might say things like, "This is the best town in the entire country! I've never met harder-working people than you! This community represents everything that makes our country great!" The townspeople, feeling proud and recognized, might respond positively, believing this politician really understands and values them.

But here's the catch—this politician may be giving the exact same speech in every town they visit, tailoring the praise to whoever is listening. The compliments aren't necessarily about genuine appreciation—they're about gaining support.

In this case, ingratiation helps the politician win over the hearts of voters by making them feel special, even though the praise is often generic and insincere. The voters, swept up in the flattery, may not question whether the politician will truly deliver on promises once in office.

Ingratiation in Religion

In religious settings, ingratiation can show up when people use their faith or devotion to gain favor within their community or with religious leaders. This can involve going above and beyond with public displays of faith, offering constant praise to religious leaders, or behaving in ways designed to appear especially righteous—all with the aim of improving one's standing in the eyes of others.

Ex: The Overly Devoted Congregant

Consider a congregant, Sam, who regularly attends church services. Every time the pastor gives a sermon, Sam is the first to stand up and praise the message, saying, "That was the most inspiring sermon I've ever heard! Your wisdom is unmatched!" Sam also volunteers for every church activity, making sure to do so in front of the pastor, and often loudly declares how much the pastor's guidance has improved his life.

At first, this might seem like genuine appreciation and dedication. But over time, others begin to notice that Sam's actions are more about being seen as the most devout member than about true faith. Sam's ingratiation earns him a special place in the pastor's circle, invitations to exclusive gatherings, and even leadership roles within the church, despite the fact that his actions may not come from genuine belief but from a desire to gain status.

In religious contexts, ingratiation can create imbalances where certain individuals gain influence or authority not because of their merit or faith but because they've manipulated others through excessive praise or public displays of devotion.

Why Do People Use Ingratiation?

Ingratiation works because everyone enjoys being liked and appreciated. People are naturally drawn to those who make them feel good about themselves, so when someone flatters us, it feels pleasant—even if the praise is overblown or insincere.

People use ingratiation for several reasons:

To gain favor: Whether in personal relationships, politics, or religion, ingratiation helps people win favor and approval from others. This can lead to advantages like special treatment, support, or influence.

To avoid conflict: In relationships, some people use ingratiation to avoid difficult conversations or disagreements. By constantly praising the other person, they sidestep confrontation, even if it means not being honest about their own feelings.

To boost status: In groups or organizations, ingratiation can be a way to climb the social ladder. By excessively praising leaders or being overly helpful, individuals can gain recognition and power within the group.

How to Recognize Ingratiation?

Recognizing ingratiation can be tricky because it often feels good to be complimented. But here are some signs that someone might be using ingratiation as a form of manipulation:

Excessive praise: Compliments are nice, but if someone is constantly showering you with praise, especially when it doesn't seem earned, it might be a red flag.

Agreeing with everything: If someone always agrees with you, even when you're clearly wrong, they may be using ingratiation to stay on your good side.

Flattery before a request: Notice if someone tends to butter you up before asking for a favor or something in return. This could be a sign that their compliments are strategic, not sincere.

Public displays of devotion: In religious or group settings, if someone goes out of their way to appear overly devoted or helpful, especially when it seems performative, they might be ingratiating themselves to gain status or recognition.

How to Respond to Ingratiation?

When you recognize that someone is using ingratiation, it's important not to fall into the trap of letting flattery cloud your judgment. Here's how to handle it:

Stay grounded: Compliments are nice, but don't let them influence important decisions. Make sure your choices are based on facts, not just feelings.

Ask for honesty: In relationships, encourage honest communication rather than constant praise. Make it clear that you value real conversations more than flattery.

Set boundaries: If you feel like someone is ingratiating themselves for personal gain, it's okay to set boundaries and not give in to their requests or manipulation.

By staying aware of how ingratiation works, we can avoid falling into its trap and ensure that our decisions and relationships are based on honesty and authenticity, not on empty flattery.

Part VI

The Chamber of Psychopaths

Why Do We Love Crime Thrillers?

Crime thrillers have become hugely popular in the past five years, especially in our country. People love watching movies and shows about famous murderers. These stories, filled with violent acts, should scare us, but somehow, they keep us hooked. We watch one shocking scene after another, feeling a mix of fear and excitement.

But imagine if a real murderer came to our village or city. We'd be terrified. Fear would spread like a dark cloud, changing how we feel about everything. Suddenly, the crimes we see on screen wouldn't seem so entertaining.

When we're sitting safely at home, though, serial killers in movies seem distant, almost unreal, like stone figures we can observe without fear. The intense scenes stay with us, playing over in our minds. But when the movie ends, and the stress fades, something interesting happens—our brain releases chemicals that make us feel relieved, even happy. It's similar to what happens when we watch a ghost movie. The fear turns into a strange kind of satisfaction.

But why are we so drawn to these stories about serial killers and crime? The answer might lie in how our brains work. We're naturally wired to pay attention to danger and scary things because, long ago, our survival depended on it. Paying attention to threats helped our ancestors stay alive.

Serial killers have existed throughout history, but we only started calling them that in the past century. Over time, experts like psychologists, neuroscientists, and criminologists have tried to figure out why we're so fascinated by these killers. But there isn't one clear answer. Many theories have been put forward, but none of them completely satisfy our curiosity. In the end, much of it is left to our imagination, with only bits of science trying to explain the rest.

Who Are Serial Killers?

Serial killers are people who commit at least three murders, but what makes them different is that they don't do it all at once. There are gaps of time between each crime, almost as if they plan their actions carefully. This isn't random violence—it's more calculated. Many serial killers are thought to have some kind of mental disorder or extreme, often disturbing, desires.

What's interesting—and chilling—is that most serial killers don't feel emotions the way we do. They don't love, they don't feel empathy, and they certainly don't feel guilty about what they've done. Even if they know it's wrong, they won't regret it. For them, laws and rules mean nothing. The pain of their victims doesn't bother them at all. In fact, some of them are driven by a desire for revenge—against certain people or sometimes even society itself.

As humans, we naturally try to find reasons behind such behavior. We assume that serial killers must have had terrible childhoods—maybe they were abused, neglected, or experienced some kind of trauma. It's easier for us to believe that something awful happened to them that pushed them down this dark path. But the truth is, not all serial killers come from such backgrounds. Some didn't suffer through abuse, and not all of them have serious mental illnesses.

The way we often imagine serial killers—broken people with tragic pasts—isn't always the reality. While some may fit that description, many don't. There's no rule that says a serial killer must have had a traumatic childhood or a severe mental disorder to become what they are.

The Most Notorious Serial Killers

1. Jack the Ripper - The Mysterious Killer

One of the most notorious and mysterious figures in human history is Jack the Ripper. His terrifying crimes took place in 1888 in the Whitechapel district of London, and even today, no one knows for sure who he was or what drove him to kill. According to official reports, Jack the Ripper murdered five women, all of whom were struggling to survive by selling their bodies. His method was chilling. He would lure the women to a secluded spot, and once alone, he would brutally attack them.

After killing his victims, he would cut open their bodies and remove certain organs like the kidneys and liver. The gruesome nature of his killings shocked the entire city, leaving a deep scar on the collective conscience of Londoners.

Despite many attempts to catch him, including the use of modern forensic science, DNA analysis, and other investigative techniques, Jack the Ripper was never found. His identity remains a mystery to this day, and he has since become one of the most infamous figures in the world of crime. Because of his horrific acts and the fact that he killed multiple victims in a similar way, Jack the Ripper is now considered one of the first known serial killers.

2. The Chilling Story of Jeffrey Dahmer

Jeffrey Dahmer's horrifying story of cannibalism and murder shook the entire city of Milwaukee, Wisconsin, and left a lasting scar on the United States. From 1978 to 1991, Dahmer killed 17 boys and young men, many of whom came from disadvantaged backgrounds. His crimes were so brutal that for years, he terrorized an entire community. People couldn't believe that someone could commit such monstrous acts.

Dahmer's disturbing behavior started at a young age. As a child, he showed signs of deep psychological problems. He was obsessed with dead animals and often collected their remains. As he grew older, his dark tendencies worsened. He struggled with alcoholism and had an uncontrollable sexual drive. Eventually, this combination of disturbing obsessions and violent impulses led him down the path of a serial killer.

Dahmer's method of luring his victims was chilling. He would approach young men in public places, offering to take their photos or inviting them back to his apartment. Once there, he gave them alcohol laced with drugs, and after they were unconscious, he would strangle them. What happened next was even more horrifying—Dahmer would have sex with the corpses and then dismember their bodies, cutting them up with the precision of a surgeon.

In his twisted mind, Dahmer didn't stop there. He would keep certain body parts, like skulls, hearts, and genitals, as gruesome trophies. He even took photographs of his victims at various stages of the killings, turning his apartment into a horrifying museum of death. Dahmer also confessed to eating parts of his victims, continuing his terrifying obsession with control and possession.

Despite the shocking nature of his crimes, Dahmer managed to avoid arrest for many years. But in 1991, the police finally caught him, and the world learned the full extent of his brutal killings. He was sentenced to prison, but in a tragic twist of fate, just two years later, Dahmer was beaten to death by a fellow inmate.

3. The Chilling Tale of Ted Bundy

Ted Bundy is often remembered as one of the most infamous serial killers in history. According to official U.S. government records, he confessed to murdering around 30 young women. However, some believe the real number could be over 100.

Born in the United States, Bundy appeared charming, intelligent, and good-looking—qualities that helped him easily attract his victims. He stood out from other serial killers in that he carefully planned his murders, often choosing college-aged women who were considered beautiful. His manipulative personality allowed him to convince these women that he was trustworthy, sometimes posing as a police officer or firefighter to lure them into his car. Once they were in his grasp, there was no escape.

Bundy's ability to evade capture made him even more terrifying. He was arrested multiple times, but each time he managed to escape, continuing his killing spree. Bundy took gruesome trophies from his victims, keeping parts of their bodies as reminders of his horrific crimes. His final victim was a 12-year-old girl, marking the end of his brutal acts. After years of terrorizing the country, Bundy was finally arrested and sentenced to death. He was executed on January 24, 1989, in Florida's electric chair, bringing an end to one of the most chilling chapters in U.S. crime history.

4. The Dark Legend of Raman Raghav

Raman Raghav, also known as Psycho Raman, was a notorious serial killer who terrorized the slums of Bombay (now Mumbai) during the 1960s. His victims were often the homeless or those living in slums, people who had nowhere to turn. Government records suggest that he killed at least 23 people, but the actual number could be much higher.

Raghav suffered from paranoid schizophrenia, a severe mental illness. People with this condition often believe strange and unbelievable things—like being watched or controlled by unseen forces. Raghav believed he was carrying out the will of some higher power, and he would stalk his victims, attacking them with an iron rod. His unpredictable behavior made him extremely difficult for the police to track down.

At the time, the lack of advanced forensic technology made it hard for investigators to connect the dots between Raghav's killings. His victims were brutally attacked, making it challenging to identify a pattern. Despite the difficulty, the Bombay police eventually caught him in 1968. His confessions were bizarre, full of delusions about divine forces guiding his actions.

Due to his mental illness, Raghav did not receive the death penalty. Instead, he was sentenced to life imprisonment, where he spent the rest of his days. He died in 1995, leaving behind a legacy of fear and confusion.

5. Charles Sobhraj - The Serpent

Once known as one of the world's most notorious serial killers, Charles Sobhraj earned the chilling nickname "The Serpent." His reputation for being cunning, slippery, and dangerous made him infamous, especially during the 1970s. He targeted

Western travelers in Asia, particularly those following the "Hippie Trail," a popular route for young people seeking spiritual and cultural experiences through places like India and Nepal.

Charles was born in 1944 in Vietnam to an Indian father and a Vietnamese mother, but he grew up in France. His childhood was troubled, full of conflicts and challenges. His parents separated early in his life, and he spent time in juvenile detention centers, where he learned many of the skills that would later help him in his criminal career.

As a young adult, Charles wanted to live a high-profile, glamorous life. To achieve this, he turned to crime, starting with car thefts and small-time scams. Over time, he expanded his operations across Europe and Asia, using his intelligence, charm, and fluency in several languages to fool people. He could adapt to any culture and situation, making him a master manipulator.

His main targets were Western tourists traveling through the hippy trail. He would charm his way into their lives by pretending to be a guide, a gem dealer, or a businessman. He gained their trust, offering them food, drinks, and luxury. But this kindness was a mask—he would poison his victims' food or drinks, leaving them weak or unconscious. He then strangled or beat them to death, earning the title "Bikini Killer" because many of his victims were found wearing swimsuits.

Charles didn't just kill for fun—he stole his victims' money, passports, and belongings, using these to continue his life on the run. He committed crimes in Thailand, India, Nepal, Malaysia, and Indonesia, always staying one step ahead of the law by using fake identities and forged passports. It's believed that he killed at least 12 people, though the true number may never be known. Many psychologists believe that Charles had a special talent for manipulating people, making them trust him before he struck.

In 1977, his luck finally ran out. He tried to poison a group of French tourists in New Delhi, but they became suspicious and alerted the police. Charles was arrested and sentenced to prison in India. However, his story didn't end there. In 1986, he managed to escape by throwing a birthday party for the prison guards and poisoning their food. He was caught soon after and remained in prison until 1997 when he was released and deported to France.

After his release, Charles became something of a celebrity in France. He sold his life story for books and interviews, enjoying the fame that came with his dark past. But in 2003, for reasons still unclear, he returned to Nepal—where he was wanted for the murders of two tourists. He was arrested once again and sentenced to 20 years in prison.

On December 21, 2021, after serving 19 years of his sentence, the Nepal Supreme Court ordered his release due to his good behavior and health issues. He returned to France, where he now lives.

6. Renuka Shinde and Seema Gavit – The Indian Yakshis

Renuka Shinde and Seema Gavit are India's first documented female serial killers, a chilling fact that contrasts sharply with the nurturing image of women. Throughout nature, it is a mother's instinct to protect her young, even at the cost of her own life. This evolutionary drive is present across species, and human mothers are no exception.

However, the story of these two women defies this fundamental instinct. How could women, traditionally seen as protectors, become torturers of children? This is a disturbing question that has left many, including psychologists, struggling to understand. Television dramas often focus on family life and the roles of women, yet here was a case where maternal instinct had been twisted beyond recognition.

Between 1990 and 1996, Renuka Shinde and Seema Gavit kidnapped and murdered 13 children, most of them under the age of five. The sheer brutality of their crimes shocked the nation, as the victims were so young and defenseless. What made these acts even more terrifying was that these murders were carried out by women, something society finds hard to comprehend.

Renuka and Seema were not born criminals, but they were raised in a world of crime. Their mother, Anjanabai Gavit, was a seasoned criminal who taught them from an early age how to steal and commit other petty crimes. They grew up in an environment devoid of compassion or morality, a place where empathy was considered weakness. Under their mother's guidance, they moved from small thefts to more sinister acts—kidnapping children.

Their method was both cunning and horrifying. The sisters would snatch children from crowded places like markets, temples, and railway stations. These kidnapped children were used as tools to distract people while they committed thefts. If a child became too difficult to control, they would be drugged.

When the sisters felt that the child was of no further use, they killed them. The methods were cruel—sometimes they would smash the child's head against a wall or drop them from heights. The bodies were discarded in public places as if they were worthless.

The sisters' crimes went unnoticed for years until 1996, when a complaint was filed in Nashik. A young girl, Kranti, went missing, and her abduction led to a police investigation. The police eventually discovered the horrific truth behind her disappearance and linked it to Renuka and Seema. The case sent shockwaves across the country. It became clear that these two women, with the help of their mother, had been carrying out a killing spree for years.

In 2001, Renuka and Seema were convicted of multiple murders. Their mother, Anjanabai, also faced charges but died during the trial. The case reached the Supreme Court, where the sisters were sentenced to death. Despite multiple appeals for mercy, their petitions were rejected, including by President Pranab Mukherjee in 2014.

However, in 2014, the Bombay High Court commuted their death sentences to life imprisonment, citing the delay in carrying out the execution. The court ruled that while their crimes were beyond horrific, they would spend the rest of their lives in prison without parole, locked away from society.

Renuka Shinde and Seema Gavit's story is a dark chapter in India's criminal history, a reminder that even the most natural instincts can be corrupted in the wrong environment. It also sheds light on the ongoing issue of child abductions in the country, where thousands of children are still taken every year, many forced into begging or worse.

7. Amarjeet Sada - The World's Youngest Serial Killer

In the quiet village of Musahari, Bihar, 1998, a boy was born into a life of poverty, one that would later be marked by unimaginable horror. Amarjeet Sada, a child like any other in appearance, went on to commit a series of crimes so chilling that they placed him in the annals of history as the world's youngest serial killer. By the age of eight, Sada had already claimed the lives of three innocent children, leaving his community, and the world, in shock.

Sada's family struggled to make ends meet, with his father working as a laborer. Their life was difficult, but no one could have predicted the darkness that lurked within the young boy. It all began in 2006, when his aunt, looking for help, left her infant child with the family while she adjusted to a new job. When Sada's mother briefly left for the market, she entrusted him with the care of his baby cousin. In an eerie twist of events, Sada found amusement in slapping and pinching the baby, but his actions quickly escalated. He strangled his cousin and buried the body under grass. When confronted, he confessed casually to his mother, sparking the first of many horrific revelations.

But this was not an isolated incident. Sada's second victim was none other than his eight-month-old sister. As his parents slept, he quietly ended her life, again showing no remorse. His family, gripped by shock and shame, kept the crimes hidden, treating these unspeakable tragedies as "family matters."

The cycle of violence culminated in 2007 with the death of a six-month-old neighbor, Kushboo. After abducting her from a school, Sada strangled her and smashed her head with a brick.

This time, the authorities became involved, but even then, it was hard to believe that a child so young could be capable of such brutality. However, when Sada led them to the baby's body, his chilling confessions could no longer be ignored.

What makes this story even more unsettling is the way Sada behaved during his interrogation. Smiling often and showing no remorse, he even bartered for biscuits in exchange for information. His emotionless confession to the killings disturbed everyone who encountered him.

Psychologists assessed the boy, diagnosing him with "conduct disorders" and noting that he derived pleasure from causing harm, a trait common to sadists. Sada's inability to grasp the difference between right and wrong set him apart as a deeply troubled child, one who had already committed heinous acts before even understanding the concept of morality.

After his arrest, Indian law prevented Sada from facing a conventional trial due to his age. Instead, he was placed in a juvenile home, where he remained until he turned 18. In 2016, Sada was released with a new identity. Today, his whereabouts are unknown, but the memory of his crimes continues to haunt those who remember the gruesome story of a child whose innocence had long vanished.

Amarjeet Sada's story is a stark reminder of the complexity of human behavior and the dark potential that can exist even in the youngest among us. His case raises difficult questions about justice, morality, and the nature of evil, especially when it comes from such an unexpected place.

Part VII

The Anti Christs' Regimes

Mass Murderers

The most notorious murderers we know are often called "serial killers"—a term used for those who kill three or more people over time. But what about those who kill hundreds, even thousands, in a single act? Do we call them extremists? Terrorists? Sometimes, they aren't even given a name. What if someone takes the lives of 20 people in one go? What do we call them?

The human brain has a tendency to search for patterns, to explain the unthinkable. When we hear of a serial killer, we assume they must have been abused or neglected, that they must suffer from some deep mental illness. Yet there are countless people who've experienced hardship and abuse without turning to murder. So, do we really understand what makes someone kill?

Our films often glorify violence, painting murderers in complex shades of gray. The hero of a movie might kill dozens of people and still be celebrated for his bravery. In one scene, the hero might collect "protection money" or avenge his loved ones by killing—yet we cheer for him. We condemn the act of murder, but sometimes, we also romanticize it.

And what about those who are responsible for the deaths of thousands, or even millions? Many of them never spend a single day in prison. Some die peacefully in their homes, others are celebrated as heroes, and some still rule nations. Should we call them serial killers? They may not have pulled the trigger themselves, but they orchestrated events that led to the deaths of countless people.

Remote Killers

Imagine this if you asked a thousand people who eat chicken regularly whether they could kill a live chicken themselves, maybe not even three would be willing to do it. Most would hesitate or refuse because it's one thing to enjoy chicken on your plate, but quite another to take the life of the bird yourself.

The moment you're faced with the reality of killing something innocent and helpless, it becomes much harder.
This idea connects to something that military psychologists have long understood—it's much easier to kill from a distance.

When a soldier presses a button to drop a bomb or launch a missile, it doesn't feel the same as standing face-to-face with the person they're harming. From far away, it's easy to detach from the pain and suffering caused. You don't see the destruction up close, you don't hear the screams, and you don't feel the life slipping away. It becomes easier to quiet your conscience because the act feels less real.

On the other hand, if you're standing in front of someone and asked to harm them, everything changes. You can see their fear, hear their voice, and witness their suffering. The human connection makes it almost unbearable to follow through. It's much harder to justify cruelty when you're staring it in the face. The more distance we put between ourselves and the consequences of our actions, the easier it becomes to carry them out. Whether it's a soldier launching an attack from miles away or a person enjoying a meal without thinking about where it came from, distance makes it easier to forget the real impact of our choices.

The Anti Christs

Throughout history, there have been individuals whose actions resulted in the deaths of millions, leaving a devastating legacy of mass murder and terror. Some operated under political ideologies, while others were driven by personal vendettas, but their impacts were felt across entire nations and beyond. Here's a journey through the chilling lives of ten figures who were instrumental in orchestrating the deaths of many.

1. Adolf Hitler (Germany)

The name Adolf Hitler is almost synonymous with genocide. As the dictator of Nazi Germany, Hitler orchestrated the Holocaust, leading to the systematic murder of 6 million Jews, alongside millions of others including Poles, Romani people, and disabled individuals. His quest for a "pure" Aryan race ignited World War II, resulting in over 70 million deaths worldwide. Hitler's rise to power through propaganda, hate, and manipulation remains one of the darkest chapters in human history.

2. Joseph Stalin (Soviet Union)

Stalin's reign of terror in the Soviet Union was marked by paranoia and brutality. His policies of collectivization and forced famine, particularly the Holodomor in Ukraine, killed millions of peasants. Stalin's Great Purge eliminated political rivals, intellectuals, and ordinary citizens through executions and gulags. It's estimated that Stalin was responsible for around 20 million deaths during his reign.

3. Pol Pot (Cambodia)

Pol Pot's Khmer Rouge regime aimed to create an agrarian socialist utopia in Cambodia, but instead it led to the deaths of approximately 2 million people, nearly a quarter of the country's population. Pol Pot's policies included forced evacuations of cities, forced labor, and mass executions. Known as the Cambodian genocide, victims included intellectuals, professionals, and ethnic minorities, marking one of the most horrific episodes of mass murder in Southeast Asia.

4. Genghis Khan (Mongol Empire)

While Genghis Khan is often revered for his military strategy and the vast Mongol Empire he created, his conquests left a trail of death and destruction. His invasions across Asia and Europe resulted in the deaths of an estimated 40 million people. Entire cities were wiped out, and Khan's ruthlessness was legendary. However, his legacy is complex, as he also united tribes and promoted trade along the Silk Road.

5. Leopold II (Belgium)

King Leopold II of Belgium personally ruled the Congo Free State as his private colony. His regime in Congo was marked by brutal exploitation, where native Congolese were forced into labor to extract rubber. Failure to meet quotas resulted in mutilations, torture, and mass killings. It's estimated that up to 10 million Congolese died under Leopold's rule. His atrocities were hidden for years, but they are now recognized as one of the worst cases of colonial exploitation.

6. Idi Amin (Uganda)

Idi Amin, the self-proclaimed "Butcher of Uganda," ruled the country with an iron fist from 1971 to 1979. His regime was marked by ethnic persecution, political repression, and widespread human rights abuses. It's estimated that Amin was responsible for the deaths of between 100,000 and 500,000 Ugandans. His brutal methods included torture and public executions, earning him a reputation as one of Africa's most infamous dictators.

7. Saddam Hussein (Iraq)

Saddam Hussein's regime in Iraq was one of oppression and violence. He is best known for his use of chemical weapons against Kurdish civilians during the Al-Anfal campaign, resulting in the deaths of tens of thousands. Additionally, his invasion of Kuwait sparked the Gulf War, and internal purges, political killings, and wars with Iran and Kuwait resulted in hundreds of thousands of deaths during his rule.

8. Kim Il-Sung (North Korea)

As the founding leader of North Korea, Kim Il-Sung established a totalitarian regime that continues under his descendants. His policies led to widespread famine, political purges, and executions. The Korean War, which Kim Il-Sung initiated, resulted in millions of deaths. His legacy is carried on by his son Kim Jong-il and grandson Kim Jong-un, under whose rule human rights violations persist, with millions suffering under the oppressive regime.

9. Heinrich Himmler (Germany)

Himmler, one of Hitler's closest associates, was the architect of the Holocaust. As the head of the SS and Gestapo, Himmler was responsible for the construction and operation of concentration camps where millions of Jews, Romani, political dissidents, and others were exterminated. His meticulous planning and chilling efficiency in carrying out genocide make him one of the deadliest figures in Nazi Germany.

These individuals used political power, manipulation, and often ideological fervor to justify mass murder on an unimaginable scale. What binds them together is their ability to dehumanize their victims, rally supporters, and create systems of oppression that led to the deaths of millions. Their legacies serve as a grim reminder of the atrocities that can arise when unchecked power meets unchecked hatred.

As we reflect on history's most notorious mass murderers like Adolf Hitler, Joseph Stalin, and Pol Pot, the scale of their crimes leaves us haunted. These men wielded power with devastating consequences, orchestrating genocides, purges, and wars that led to the loss of millions of innocent lives. Hitler's Holocaust wiped out six million Jews; Stalin's purges and forced famines starved millions; Pol Pot's Khmer Rouge brutalized an entire nation.

Yet, history continues to glorify other figures, like Napoleon and Alexander the Great, despite their own roles in mass deaths through conquest and war.

Even today, the pattern of mass violence persists. As I write this book, a swift genocide is unfolding in West Asia, with the

Western powers—who often claim to be the guardians of justice—fueling the violence by shipping weapons into conflict zones. Innocent children, newborns, pregnant women, and the disabled are among the casualties. The irony is chilling war is waged in the name of terrorism, yet it often results in the mass murder of civilians.

History, it seems, is written by the victors, who selectively highlight their conquests while sweeping under the rug the atrocities committed in their name. The list of mass murderers will never truly end, as long as we continue to glorify power and overlook the innocent lives crushed beneath it.

Part VIII

The Lynching Gallery

The Satanic Crowds

In 1896, French social psychologist Gustave Le Bon published a book that would forever change the way we understand group behavior. Titled "The Crowd A Study of the Popular Mind," Le Bon's work explained how individuals could undergo a complete transformation when they become part of a large, emotional crowd. According to Le Bon, people lose their sense of self when they merge into a crowd. They forget their social status, their occupation, their values, and even their sense of right and wrong.

In a crowd, ordinary people can suddenly do things they would never consider when alone. These might be acts of violence, cruelty, or destruction—actions completely at odds with their usual behavior. How does this happen? It's as if their individual identity disappears, absorbed into the collective identity of the crowd. This is why people who are kind, thoughtful, and peaceful in everyday life can become part of a violent mob, abandoning their sense of civility and reverting to a more primal state of mind.

When Feelings Spread Like Fire

One of the main reasons people act differently in crowds is a psychological phenomenon called emotional contagion. In simple terms, emotions are contagious. If you're surrounded by fear, anger, or excitement, you're likely to start feeling those same emotions yourself. This is why crowds can quickly spiral out of control.

Imagine a protest that begins peacefully. But as emotions heat up, people start shouting, pushing, and behaving aggressively.

Soon, what started as a peaceful gathering has turned into a riot. The shared emotion of the group amplifies, spreading like wildfire. People in the crowd lose their individual restraint, swept up in the collective energy of the moment. This is how crowd violence can start, and it's why ordinary people can find themselves committing acts they would never do on their own.

The Power of a Common Cause

Crowds don't just come together randomly. Often, people gather because they share a strong emotional bond over a particular issue. This is what social psychologists refer to as emergent norm theory—the idea that people come together not just as individuals, but because they are united by a shared emotional drive.

Take, for example, the sensitive issue of cow slaughter in India. The mere rumor of such an act can unite people from different backgrounds and spur them to violent action. These individuals may not have been violent before, but when they come together over a shared cause, their collective emotion pushes them to extremes.

Feeling Invisible in a Crowd

Another key factor in crowd behavior is the sense of anonymity that comes from being part of a large group. When people feel anonymous, they also feel a sense of security—they believe they won't be recognized or held accountable for their actions. This feeling of safety can lead people to do things they would never do in public or alone. They feel protected by the crowd, hidden in plain sight.

Often, those who incite or lead mob violence may have darker intentions or even criminal histories. But the majority of people who join a violent mob are often regular individuals—students, workers, or young people—who get caught up in the moment and make impulsive, dangerous decisions.

The Dark Side of Mob Justice

History is filled with examples of wild justice—when crowds take the law into their own hands, bypassing the legal system and deciding guilt and punishment on the spot. One haunting example comes from Haiti, where, after an earthquake, rumors spread that voodoo priests were responsible for an epidemic. Without waiting for any legal process, mobs executed 45 priests, convinced that they were the cause of the disaster.

This kind of mob justice is not limited to one place or culture. In Nigeria, there exists a similar phenomenon known as jungle justice, where people accused of crimes are brutally punished by mobs, often without any trial. In both cases, the mob believes they are acting righteously, even though their actions are driven by emotion rather **than facts.**

The "Holy Shudder"

The idea of committing a violent act, especially in the name of justice, is something that has long puzzled psychologists. Nobel Prize-winning zoologist Konrad Lorenz studied violent behavior in both animals and humans, and he described what he called a "holy shudder"—a sensation that some people experience before committing acts of violence. It's as though they perceive their actions not as crimes, but as heroic acts, done for the protection or benefit of their community. This feeling of righteousness, mixed with the collective energy of a crowd, can push people to commit terrible acts, all the while believing they are doing something virtuous.

When Man Becomes Savage

Two famous social psychologists, Dr. Philip Zimbardo and Stanley Milgram, conducted groundbreaking experiments to understand how ordinary people can turn savage under the right circumstances. Zimbardo's Stanford Prison Experiment, conducted in 1971, showed how quickly people in positions of power can become cruel. Students who played the role of prison guards began abusing their peers who were cast as prisoners, simply because they were given authority and power.

Similarly, Milgram's experiments on obedience revealed that people are capable of inflicting harm on others if they believe they are following orders or that their actions are sanctioned by authority figures. These studies show that anyone can be driven to cruelty and violence under the right conditions—especially in a crowd, where responsibility is diffused and consequences seem distant.

The Dangers of the Crowd

Every day, somewhere in the world, someone is being lynched by a mob. Whether it's physical violence or online harassment, crowd psychology can turn ordinary people into participants in horrific acts. As Dr. Zimbardo pointed out, we all have the potential to be cruel—it just takes the right situation to unlock it.

The lesson is clear when we find ourselves swept up in the emotions of a crowd, we must take a step back and think for ourselves. Are we acting out of fear, anger, or a desire to belong? Or are we following our own sense of justice and morality? Because once the crowd takes over, it's easy to lose sight of who we really are.

Part IX

The Artistic Genies

The Confident Genies

A con artist is someone who masterfully deceives others, often by winning their trust, only to exploit it for personal gain—usually money or valuable assets. The term itself comes from "confidence" (con), highlighting how these individuals skillfully gain the confidence of their victims, and "artist," representing their craft in deception. Con artists use manipulation, charm, and calculated tactics to make their schemes seem legitimate, only for the victim to realize too late that they've been duped.

Con artists, whether working alone or as part of a larger scheme, often target their victims' emotions, playing on greed, fear, or even sympathy. Their skill lies in making lies seem like truth, often through elaborate stories or too-good-to-be-true promises. While "con man" is commonly used for male fraudsters, "con artist" applies broadly to anyone—regardless of gender—who thrives on deception for personal profit

Imagine meeting someone who offers you a deal that seems like a once-in-a-lifetime opportunity. They might present themselves as a wealthy investor, a long-lost relative, or someone with insider knowledge about a booming business. Slowly, they weave their story, gaining your trust, and before you know it, you're hooked. You think you've struck gold—until the money, or they themselves, vanish into thin air.

Con artists have existed for centuries, from the classic "snake oil salesmen" to today's digital scammers. What makes them so dangerous is not just their skill in deception, but the way they exploit the deepest vulnerabilities of their victims. Whether it's in a personal relationship, a business deal, or a charity scam, they create a world that feels so real until it crashes down, leaving people devastated and questioning how they could have ever been fooled.

I. Elizabeth Holmes

Once upon a time, Elizabeth Holmes was hailed as the next Steve Jobs, a young visionary who promised to change the world of healthcare. She founded Theranos, a company that claimed it could run hundreds of blood tests from a single drop of blood, revolutionizing the medical industry. It was a dream that sounded too good to be true, but Holmes made people believe in it. By 2015, she was the youngest self-made female billionaire in America, and Theranos was valued at an astonishing $9 billion. But beneath the surface, this dream was built on deception.

Crafting the Perfect Image

Holmes didn't just create a company; she created a story. She told the world that her fear of needles as a child inspired her to invent a better way to test blood. People loved this narrative—who wouldn't want a world where a single finger prick could replace painful blood draws? Holmes wore black turtlenecks, imitating Steve Jobs, and spoke with a deep, unwavering voice, selling not just her product, but herself as the face of innovation.

To give her venture credibility, Holmes surrounded herself with powerful figures. Her board included former U.S. Secretaries of State Henry Kissinger and George Shultz, and even media titan Rupert Murdoch invested millions. These connections made it hard for anyone to doubt her. If such influential people believed in her, how could she be wrong?

Holmes kept Theranos in "stealth mode" for years, revealing little about how the technology worked. This secrecy built intrigue and, in the world of Silicon Valley, intrigue often means success.

Building a House of Cards

Behind closed doors, however, the truth was far darker. Theranos wasn't the revolutionary company it claimed to be. Holmes had created a toxic environment where employees were too afraid to speak out. Those who raised concerns were silenced or fired. She avoided sharing the technical details of her blood-testing machine, the Edison, which, as it turned out, didn't work. Instead, the company relied on commercially available machines from other companies, but even then, the results were often inaccurate.

Holmes used every trick in the book to keep the illusion alive. She appeared on magazine covers, struck high-profile deals with Walgreens, and delivered confident speeches. But when journalists, like John Carreyrou from *The Wall Street Journal*, started asking questions, Holmes didn't back down. She aggressively threatened lawsuits and tried to silence her critics, hoping to keep the truth buried.

When the Truth Came Out

Eventually, the cracks became too big to ignore. Investigations revealed that Holmes had lied about everything—from the capabilities of her technology to the company's financials. The U.S. Department of Defense deals she had boasted about didn't exist, and revenue figures were grossly inflated. The truth was, Theranos's "breakthrough" device was a complete failure.

By 2018, the entire operation had collapsed. Holmes was charged with fraud for deceiving investors out of more than $700 million. She went from being a billionaire to having nothing. The company was dissolved, and Holmes was banned from serving as an officer of a public company for a decade.

Why Didn't We See It Coming?

After Theranos's fall, many people claimed they "always knew" it was too good to be true. But hindsight is a tricky thing. During her rise, Holmes's image was so perfectly crafted that few saw through the façade. People wanted to believe in her dream. Investors feared missing out on the next big thing, and her powerful connections made it easy for them to ignore red flags.

Hindsight bias made it seem obvious in retrospect, but the reality was far more complex. Holmes had manipulated not just individuals, but a system built on trust, ambition, and the desire to be part of something groundbreaking.

A Dream Turned Nightmare

Elizabeth Holmes's story isn't just about a failed company. It's about how easily people can be misled when they want to believe in something. She didn't just sell a product—she sold a dream. And that dream, wrapped in ambition and deceit, eventually became one of Silicon Valley's greatest nightmares. Holmes's rise and fall serve as a cautionary tale of how charisma and manipulation can blind even the smartest minds to the truth, until it's too late.

II. Victor Lustig

Victor Lustig was no ordinary criminal. He was a master of deception, a con artist whose audacity made him one of the most legendary tricksters of the early 20th century. His name became famous for one daring act above all selling the Eiffel Tower. Twice. But that was just one of many scams Lustig pulled off, playing on people's greed, fear, and desire for status, leading them into his intricate web of lies.

The Eiffel Tower Scam

It was 1925, and Lustig was in Paris when he came across a news article that sparked a brilliant idea. The article talked about how expensive it was to maintain the Eiffel Tower, and there was even talk of dismantling it. To Lustig, this wasn't just news—it was an opportunity. He quickly hatched a plan to do the unthinkable sell the Eiffel Tower for scrap.

Armed with fake government papers, Lustig posed as a high-ranking official from the French Ministry of Posts and Telegraphs. He invited a group of scrap metal dealers to a luxurious hotel for a secret meeting. With charm and confidence, he explained that the French government was quietly trying to sell the Eiffel Tower to reduce costs. The sale had to be kept secret because of its controversial nature, and Lustig, as the supposed man in charge, was responsible for selecting the right buyer.

Among the dealers was André Poisson, a businessman desperate to make a name for himself in Paris. Lustig, always a keen judge of character, knew Poisson was the perfect target. In a private meeting, Lustig hinted that a bribe could help secure the deal. Poisson, eager to rise in social status, paid Lustig a large sum—70,000 francs—for the rights to the Eiffel Tower.

With the money in hand, Lustig fled to Austria, correctly predicting that Poisson would be too embarrassed to report the scam to the police. After all, who would admit to buying the Eiffel Tower?

Lustig, emboldened by his success, returned to Paris a few months later and tried to pull off the same con with another group of scrap dealers. But this time, one of them grew suspicious and alerted the police. Lustig, ever the smooth operator, escaped to the United States before they could catch him.

Making Money Out of Thin Air

But Lustig's genius didn't stop at selling monuments. He also had a knack for inventing elaborate scams, and one of his most infamous was the "Rumanian Box." This device, a beautifully crafted mahogany box, supposedly had the power to duplicate money.

Lustig would perform demonstrations, placing a real high-denomination bill into the box along with blank paper. After a few hours, the box would produce an identical bill—at least that's what the victim thought. In reality, Lustig had pre-loaded the box with real bills, making the illusion flawless.
Convinced by the demonstration, victims would pay huge amounts to buy the "money-printing" machine, believing they could make endless amounts of cash. Lustig, always planning ahead, packed the box with a few more real bills to buy himself time before disappearing with their money.

One of Lustig's most notable victims was a Texas sheriff, who was so impressed by the box that he tracked Lustig down in Chicago to buy it. When the sheriff eventually realized he'd been conned, he was furious and went after Lustig. But even then, Lustig was one step ahead. He convinced the sheriff that the problem wasn't the box—it was the sheriff's own incompetence. To smooth things over, Lustig "compensated" him with counterfeit bills.

This clever move worked for a while, but it was also Lustig's undoing. The counterfeiting scheme eventually caught the attention of federal authorities, and it wasn't long before the law finally caught up with the legendary conman.

The Legacy of a Master Conman

Victor Lustig's scams were more than just about stealing money—they were elaborate performances where he played on human nature. People wanted to believe they could buy something as outrageous as the Eiffel Tower or own a machine that printed money. Lustig gave them what they wanted, and in doing so, he became one of history's most audacious and fascinating criminals. Even though he was eventually caught, his legacy as the man who sold the Eiffel Tower twice lives on as a testament to the power of deception.

Victor Lustig was no stranger to manipulating the weak or the desperate, but one of his boldest moves was conning someone who few would dare to cross Al Capone, one of the most feared and ruthless criminals in America. Lustig's audacity knew no limits, and it was this fearlessness that made him legendary.

Fooling the Untouchable

Lustig's scheme to swindle Al Capone wasn't your typical con—it was a game of patience and cunning. He approached Capone with a crooked deal, convincing the gangster to invest $50,000 in a supposedly foolproof venture. Capone, always hungry for profit, agreed and handed over the money.

For two months, Lustig held onto the cash without making a move. Then, instead of disappearing or inventing some grand excuse, Lustig did something that threw Capone completely off guard—he returned the full $50,000, claiming the deal had fallen through. Lustig explained that he couldn't in good conscience keep the money and that his integrity was more important than any profit.

Capone, a man who had seen every trick in the book, was impressed. Here was a man, in his eyes, who could have run off with his money but chose to do the "honorable" thing instead. Seeing Lustig as trustworthy, Capone rewarded him with $5,000 for his honesty. What Capone didn't know was that this was Lustig's plan all along—the conman had never intended to run a deal; he just wanted that reward. And in classic Lustig fashion, he got it, all without Capone ever suspecting a thing.

Betrayed by Love

But even a master manipulator like Victor Lustig couldn't outrun fate forever. During the Great Depression, Lustig expanded his operations, turning to large-scale counterfeiting. He flooded the U.S. with thousands of fake dollars each month, which eventually caught the attention of the federal government. But it wasn't his counterfeit bills that led to his capture—it was a broken heart.

Lustig's long-time mistress, angry after discovering that he had left her for another woman, decided to betray him. In a fit of jealousy and revenge, she tipped off the authorities, and soon after, Lustig was arrested in 1935.

Even behind bars, Lustig's knack for deception didn't fade. He feigned ignorance, trying to charm his way out of trouble. In a final daring move, he even managed to escape from a federal detention center, showing once again his flair for the dramatic. But the law caught up with him, and this time, there was no escape. Lustig was sentenced to 20 years in Alcatraz.

The Final Act

Victor Lustig, who had sold the Eiffel Tower, duped some of the richest men in the world, and even fooled Al Capone, spent his final years behind bars. He died of pneumonia in 1947, leaving behind a legacy as one of the most skilled con artists of all time.

Lustig's life is a testament to how far charm, wit, and manipulation can take you. He had an uncanny ability to read people—whether it was selling an iconic landmark or fooling a notorious gangster, Lustig knew exactly how to play on people's emotions, desires, and fears. His marks were often left feeling like they were getting the better end of the deal, when in reality, Lustig had already won the game long before they even realized they were playing.

Even today, his story serves as a reminder of how easily people can be led astray by their own hopes and greed. Victor Lustig wasn't just selling cons—he was selling dreams, and for a time, the world bought them.

III. Frank William Abagnale Jr

Frank William Abagnale Jr. was born on April 27, 1948, in the Bronx, New York. His childhood was anything but smooth. At 15, his parents divorced, and he ended up living with his father and stepmother in Mount Vernon, New York. It was around this time that young Frank pulled off his first con.

Armed with a gasoline credit card his father had given him, Frank racked up a shocking $3,400 bill. His little scheme got him sent to a reform school. Not long after, in December 1964, Frank, eager for adventure, joined the U.S. Navy at just 16. His time there didn't last long—three months later, he was discharged, and soon after, arrested for petty theft.

Frank's ability to deceive others was about to get much more serious. In March 1965, he tried impersonating a police officer, but when the woman he approached grew suspicious and called the real police, Frank was caught with a toy gun and fake badge. This was just the beginning of his wild journey.

By June 1965, Frank's crimes escalated. He was arrested by the FBI in California for stealing a neighbor's Ford Mustang and funding his cross-country trip with stolen checks. This marked the start of his transformation into one of the most famous con artists ever.

At 17, Frank hatched an audacious plan to pose as a commercial airline pilot. He forged checks to buy a pilot's uniform and even managed to convince people he had graduated from a prestigious pilot school. However, this charade didn't last long. He was arrested for check theft just days later and sentenced to three years in prison.

But Frank wasn't ready to give up his con game. After his early release, he took on a new identity—this time, as a TWA pilot in Louisiana. He charmed his way into the lives of a local family, staying in their home and pretending to be a pilot and a social worker. However, his lies caught up with him when a suspicious reverend contacted the airline to check his story.

Frank was arrested again, facing charges of theft and forgery. His adventures weren't limited to the U.S. Frank's cons continued across Europe. In September 1969, he was arrested in France for car theft and fraud. After serving time in French and Swedish prisons, he was deported back to the United States in 1970, but his life of deception was far from over.

Back in the U.S., Frank slipped into another pilot's uniform and set up a fake stewardess recruitment scheme on college campuses. He even conducted bogus physical exams for the women he recruited, convincing everyone he was a Pan Am pilot. His scam fell apart when he was arrested again for check forgery, and although he escaped from jail, he was recaptured in New York City.

In 1971, Frank was sentenced to 12 years in prison but served just two before being paroled. After his release, he tried to go straight, even offering banks his expertise in fraud prevention. For a fee, he promised to teach them how con artists worked. This clever move launched a new career as a speaker and consultant, though Frank still exaggerated his past in his talks, claiming he'd been everything from a pediatrician to a professor.

By the late 1970s, Frank had become something of a celebrity, sharing his outrageous stories on TV shows and in interviews. His life was immortalized in the book *Catch Me If You Can*, which Steven Spielberg turned into a blockbuster movie starring Leonardo DiCaprio in 2002. True to his flair for drama, Frank made a cameo in the film as a French police officer.

Today, Frank Abagnale Jr. is known for his past as one of the world's most infamous con artists, but he's also built a new legacy as an expert in fraud prevention, advising companies on how to protect themselves from the tricks he once mastered.

IV. Mithilesh Kumar Srivastava

Natwarlal, born Mithilesh Kumar Srivastava in 1912, was India's most infamous conman, known for his incredible ability to manipulate, deceive, and repeatedly escape justice. His legendary scams included "selling" India's most iconic landmarks—the Taj Mahal, the Red Fort, Rashtrapati Bhavan, and even the Parliament House—often to gullible foreigners who were none the wiser.

Growing up in the village of Bangra in Bihar as the son of a railway station master, Natwarlal discovered his knack for forgery early on. He got his start when a neighbor sent him to deposit bank drafts, and he realized how easy it was to forge signatures. He withdrew 1,000 rupees from the neighbor's account and fled to Calcutta, where he enrolled in a commerce degree and dabbled as a casual stockbroker. Despite his various ventures, his natural talent lay in con artistry, and he eventually found himself drawn back into the world of deception.

Natwarlal's early schemes took advantage of his knowledge of the railway freight industry, banking rules, and a remarkable talent for forging signatures—even those of famous personalities. He was first arrested in 1937 for stealing nine tonnes of iron, but this didn't slow him down. Switching tactics, he briefly resorted to drugging prostitutes to steal their valuables, but soon returned to his preferred methods of fraud.

Using over fifty aliases and countless disguises, Natwarlal swindled lakhs of rupees from shop owners, bankers, and wealthy industrialists, including the likes of the Tatas, the Birlas, and Dhirubhai Ambani. One of his most elaborate scams involved defrauding Punjab National Bank of 6.5 lakhs of rupees through a clever ruse involving rail freight and bags of rice. He paid his victims with fake cheques and demand drafts, often posing as a business manager, purchasing officer, or even a well-meaning social worker. His tricks were so convincing that he allegedly once "sold" the entire Indian Parliament House, complete with its members, to an unsuspecting foreigner.

Natwarlal's charm and cunning made him a Robin Hood-like figure in his village, Bangra, where he would occasionally return to distribute his ill-gotten gains among the poor. On one occasion, he threw a lavish feast for the entire village, handing out 100 rupees to each poor villager before vanishing once again into the shadows.

Despite facing numerous charges and being sentenced to 113 years in prison across multiple cases of forgery, Natwarlal proved impossible to contain. He was arrested nine or ten times, but his escapes were legendary. In 1957, he broke out of Kanpur jail by donning a police uniform, bribing guards with a suitcase he claimed was filled with money, and casually walking out the front gate—his "bribe" was nothing more than a stack of newspapers.

Natwarlal's final arrest came in 1996 when he was 84 years old. Even then, bound to a wheelchair, he managed one last vanishing act. While being transported by police from Kanpur jail to a hospital in New Delhi, he simply disappeared at the railway station and was never seen again. His life of crime, marked by elaborate cons, brilliant misdirection, and repeated escapes, cemented his legacy as India's greatest trickster—one whose true fate remains as mysterious as the many cons he pulled.

V. Sukesh Chandrashekhar

Sukesh Chandrashekhar, a man with an extraordinary gift for manipulation, ran one of the largest extortion rackets India has ever seen. What makes his story even more shocking is that he did it all while sitting behind bars in Tihar Jail. Born in Bengaluru, Sukesh came from a humble background but always dreamed of living a life of luxury. His ambition drove him to try his hand at real estate and even car racing, but his true talent was in conning people.

From a young age, Sukesh had a knack for deception. At just 17, he fooled people into believing he was someone important. He even carried a fake letter, supposedly from the Bengaluru police commissioner, that gave him special privileges on the road. His first big scam came in 2007 when he cheated a businessman out of Rs 1.15 crore.

That was just the beginning. Sukesh became known for impersonating powerful figures, like the son of a Chief Minister, a high-ranking official from the Prime Minister's Office, and even a Supreme Court judge. His ability to trick people earned him more than 30 criminal cases. He scammed over 100 people, including politicians, leaving a trail of victims and stolen money wherever he went.

One of his biggest cons was when he extorted Rs 200 crores from Aditi Singh, the wife of former Ranbaxy promoter Shivinder Singh. Posing as a government official, Sukesh promised her that he could help get her husband out of jail. Aditi believed him, and Sukesh walked away with an enormous sum of money. But his daring didn't stop there—he also swindled Rs 50 crores from AIADMK's TTV Dhinakaran, pretending to bribe Election Commission officials.

Despite being arrested multiple times, Sukesh never let that slow him down. Every time he got out on bail, he went right back to his old ways, pulling off new scams with the same boldness.

Sukesh wasn't alone in his schemes. In 2010, he met Leena Paulose, an actress and model, who became his partner in crime. Even though Leena knew about his illegal activities, she chose to join him. The two got married in 2015 and together ran a Ponzi scheme that defrauded over 450 investors. Leena was arrested alongside Sukesh in many of his cases.

Sukesh's love for Bollywood also played a big part in his life.

He wooed actress Jacqueline Fernandez with extravagant gifts—designer bags, jewelry, luxury watches, a horse worth Rs 52 lakhs, and even four cats! Jacqueline admitted to receiving these gifts, though she claimed they hadn't met since Sukesh's arrest in 2021. Still, Sukesh continued to reach out to her, even sending her a birthday letter from jail.

Sukesh's luxurious lifestyle was like something out of a movie. He owned sixteen high-end cars, including Rolls Royce, Bentley, and Ferrari, all of which were seized from his bungalow in Chennai. His ability to manipulate and deceive people allowed him to live like a millionaire, even while sitting in a prison cell.

Sukesh Chandrashekhar's story is one of ambition without limits—a man who used his talent for deception to climb to the top, no matter how many people he had to trick along the way.

VI. Charles Ponzi

William Thompson wasn't just any thief—he was a master at fooling people, and one of the first "confidence men" in American history. In the early 1800s, Thompson walked the streets of New York with a simple but genius plan to trick wealthy people. He didn't hide in the shadows or snatch things from people's pockets. Instead, he used one powerful tool trust.

Thompson wasn't like other criminals. He dressed well, spoke politely, and acted like someone you'd want to be friends with. His whole game was about making people believe in him. And once they did, he'd trick them into giving him their valuables—willingly.

The Art of Trust

Thompson's trick was clever and bold. He would start a friendly conversation with a wealthy person on a busy street or in a fancy place. With his charming smile and smooth talk, he made people feel comfortable around him. As the conversation went on, his target would begin to trust him. That's when Thompson made his move.

He would ask for a favor—something that seemed small and innocent. "Can I borrow your watch for a moment?" or "Could you lend me a little money? I'll return it soon." His charm made the request seem so natural that the person would hand over their watch or money without thinking twice. After all, who wants to seem rude or distrustful?

The Perfect Scam

The brilliance of Thompson's scam was how simple it was. Once he had the item, he would smile, thank his target warmly, and walk away—never to return. No threats, no violence, just the power of suggestion and trust. His victims often didn't realize they'd been tricked until much later. By then, Thompson had already moved on to his next target, repeating the same routine with the same confident smile.

Thompson's scams were so famous that newspapers began calling him a "confidence man," or "con man" for short. His trick wasn't about force—it was about persuasion. He used people's natural desire to trust others, and their fear of appearing rude, against them. This was a new kind of criminal, one who relied on human nature to pull off his crimes.

The Downfall

Eventually, Thompson's luck ran out. One of his victims reported him to the police, and he was arrested. In court, the newspapers gave him the title "Confidence Man," a label that would forever define tricksters and scammers like him. Even during his trial, Thompson stayed calm, acting as confident as ever, as if he was still in control of the situation.

The Legacy

William Thompson's story didn't end with his arrest. The term "con man" became part of history, symbolizing the power of deception and the clever manipulation of trust. His scams were a lesson in how simple tricks could be just as powerful as any weapon. By playing on people's trust and kindness, Thompson showed that sometimes the most dangerous criminals aren't the ones who use force, but the ones who make you believe in them—if only for a moment.

VII. Anna Delvey

Anna Delvey, whose real name is Anna Sorokin, became famous not for being a rich socialite, but for pretending to be one. She was a master of deception, tricking some of the wealthiest people and most exclusive places in New York City into believing she was a millionaire heiress. But behind the glamorous façade was a woman who was pulling off one of the most elaborate scams the city had ever seen.

The Dream of Wealth and Fame

Anna wasn't born into riches. She grew up in a middle-class family in Russia and moved to Germany with her parents when she was a teenager. But Anna dreamed of a different life—a life of luxury, wealth, and power. So when she moved to New York in 2013, she created a new identity for herself. She became Anna Delvey, a glamorous European heiress with a fortune waiting for her in overseas bank accounts.

Anna's story was simple, yet convincing. She told people her family was incredibly wealthy, and that she was in New York to launch an art foundation that would change the city's cultural landscape. The key to her scam was confidence—she always acted like she belonged in the world of the rich and famous.

Living the Lie

Anna lived like she was already a millionaire. She stayed in expensive hotels, ate at the finest restaurants, and wore designer clothes. But the truth was, she didn't have the money to pay for any of it. She would often promise that a wire transfer was coming or that her family's "trust fund" was taking care of the bills. This lie bought her time as she moved from one hotel to another, leaving behind unpaid bills.

What made Anna's scam so successful was her ability to blend in. She hung out with the rich, attended high-society events, and convinced everyone she met that she was one of them. She would pick up the tab at dinners or order expensive bottles of champagne, always giving the impression that money was no object. But behind the scenes, she was borrowing money from friends, charming her way into private clubs, and sweet-talking hotel staff to give her credit.

The Big Scam

Anna's biggest plan was to open an exclusive art club in Manhattan. She envisioned a luxurious space where artists, celebrities, and the ultra-wealthy could gather. To make this dream a reality, she needed investors, and that's when the real con began.

Anna approached banks and wealthy investors, convincing them to loan her millions of dollars to fund her art foundation. She showed them fake financial documents, pretending she had access to a $60 million trust fund. Her charm and confidence were so convincing that one bank almost gave her $22 million for the project. In the meantime, she continued living her high-end lifestyle, staying at fancy hotels and flying on private jets, all on borrowed or stolen money.

Cracks in the Façade

But eventually, the lies started to catch up with Anna. Hotels began to demand payment for her growing bills, and friends she had borrowed money from started asking questions. One of her closest friends, Rachel Williams, was left with a $62,000 bill after a luxury trip to Morocco that Anna promised she would pay for but never did.

In 2017, Anna's web of lies began to unravel. She was arrested after failing to pay tens of thousands of dollars to hotels and banks. Her trial in 2019 was a spectacle—Anna arrived in court wearing designer outfits and still acted like the wealthy socialite she had always pretended to be. But in the end, she was convicted of multiple charges, including grand larceny and theft of services.

The Legacy of a Con

Anna Delvey's story became a media sensation, with people

fascinated by how far she went to create her fake life. She had fooled some of New York's wealthiest people, lived in luxury for years without paying a dime, and almost pulled off a multi-million-dollar scam. But in the end, her deception couldn't last forever.

Anna was sentenced to four to twelve years in prison, but even after her conviction, she remained unapologetic. In interviews, she expressed little regret, and her bold attitude only added to the public's fascination with her story.

Part X

The Professional Devils

Professional Killers

When we think of the most dangerous individuals in society, serial killers often come to mind. They're notorious for their gruesome, often unprovoked murders, driven by personal psychological disorders or desires. But there's another group that might be even more chilling—professional killers. These individuals murder not out of compulsion, but as a cold, calculated business. Unlike serial killers, who are driven by internal urges, professional killers are motivated by money, power, or control. This makes them some of the most dangerous and morally bankrupt people in society.

The Calculated Nature

Professional killers, also known as hitmen or contract killers, lack the emotional or psychological triggers that often characterize serial killers. Their killings are transactional. A hitman doesn't choose a victim out of personal obsession; they kill because someone has paid them to. This level of detachment, where a human life is reduced to a paycheck, is what makes them particularly insidious.

Consider the notorious story of Richard Kuklinski, also known as "The Iceman," who was a contract killer for the mafia. Kuklinski's murders weren't personal—he had no vendetta against his victims. To him, they were just part of the job. His cold, remorseless attitude toward killing made him far more dangerous than a typical serial killer. He was methodical, calculated, and emotionless, able to carry out murders without remorse or hesitation. In fact, Kuklinski killed over 200 people during his career as a hitman, making him one of the most prolific professional killers in history.

In Organized Crime

Professional killers often work within organized crime syndicates or political factions. The Mafia, drug cartels, and extremist political groups all employ hitmen to eliminate enemies, silence witnesses, or intimidate rivals. These killers operate within a system where death is just a tool for maintaining power. The sheer scale of the murders they commit makes them far more dangerous than lone serial killers.

Take, for example, the Mexican drug cartels. These organizations routinely hire professional killers to eliminate rivals, law enforcement officers, and even innocent civilians who might stand in their way. The infamous cartel hitman Edgar Valdez Villarreal, known as "La Barbie," was one such figure. His calculated brutality left hundreds dead, and unlike a typical serial killer, his victims weren't chosen because of personal grudges—they were simply in the way of his employers.

Worse Than Serial Killers

Serial killers often act alone, driven by personal demons or psychological issues. While their actions are horrific, they typically don't kill as part of a larger system. Professional killers, on the other hand, are part of a well-oiled machine. Their actions are often part of a broader agenda—whether it's to maintain power in organized crime, eliminate political enemies, or further their employers' financial interests.

This systemic nature makes professional killers worse than serial killers. Serial killers may be driven by internal, uncontrollable compulsions, but professional killers operate in a world where murder is business as usual. They are not outliers in society—they work within it, often shielded by the organizations they serve.

Professional killers are some of the most dangerous people in society. Unlike serial killers, whose motivations are personal and often driven by mental illness, professional killers operate with calculated detachment. Their work is transactional, and human life is reduced to a business deal. Whether working for organized crime, political groups, or simply for financial gain, their actions are often part of a broader system of violence and control.

In a world where murder becomes a commodity, and killing is just another job, professional killers represent the darkest side of humanity. They are far worse than serial killers because their actions are not isolated—professional killers are part of a machine that thrives on violence, corruption, and death.

Part XI

The Devils in Uniform

Licensed to Kill

What's the worst crime against humanity? It's not always committed by the obvious villains but sometimes by those who are supposed to protect us—the police. Imagine the despair of people who find themselves locked in police custody, tortured, broken, and silenced. These are ordinary citizens, taxpayers who help fund the very salaries of the officers who turn against them. Yet, do we call these officers murderers? No, because the law shields them, not the victims.

To grasp the depth of this injustice, just look at India's Lok Sabha. Recently, the Union government revealed an alarming statistic in the span of just two years, 4,484 people died in police custody. The state of Uttar Pradesh holds the tragic record for the highest number of these deaths, but it's a problem that haunts all corners of the country. In 2022 alone, over 2,500 cases of documented custodial violence were recorded. That's more than 2,500 lives destroyed by the very system meant to protect them.

These figures, shared by Union Minister of State for Home Affairs Nityanand Rai, are likely only a fraction of the true scale. The actual numbers are far worse. Some reports suggest that about 90 people die annually in police custody—that's roughly one death every five days. It's a cycle of brutality that seems never-ending.

Take the case of a 25-year-old man from Chennai. Arrested in April for possession of marijuana, he was dead the very next day. Experts pointed to custodial torture as the cause. Then there was Ambadipudi Mariyamma, a 40-year-old woman from the Mala caste, accused of robbery. She never left police custody alive, her body a testament to the abuse she endured.

In theory, the justice system tells us that "it is better that one hundred guilty persons should escape than that one innocent person should suffer." Yet, in reality, innocent lives are lost behind closed doors—often at the hands of those who are supposed to uphold the law. These people die nameless, their stories drowned out by bureaucracy and the heavy silence of impunity.

The law, it seems, offers a license to kill, as long as the uniform is blue and the brutality happens in the shadows.

Part XII

The Unholy Extortion

Holy Hells

Religion, at its core, is meant to be a guiding force, offering people hope, purpose, and a moral compass. For many, faith provides a sense of belonging and a framework for navigating life's challenges. However, there is a troubling side to this story—one where individuals use religion as a tool for manipulation, extortion, and, in extreme cases, violence.

The Art of Manipulation

Some religious leaders, self-proclaimed prophets, or so-called "demigods" take advantage of the deep faith people have. They position themselves as chosen individuals with divine authority, claiming they have special knowledge or a direct connection to a higher power. Through carefully crafted sermons, charismatic speeches, or even "miracles," these figures create an aura of holiness around themselves.

They often promise blessings, prosperity, or even eternal life to their followers, but there's always a catch. To achieve these rewards, followers are convinced they must give something in return—money, property, or absolute loyalty. This manipulation isn't just about financial gain. Some leaders use their influence to control their followers' lives, pushing them to make choices they would never have considered otherwise.

Extortion in the Name of Faith

One of the most troubling aspects of this manipulation is how it leads to extortion. Followers, believing they are doing God's will, are often pressured into giving vast sums of money or valuables to their religious leaders. This extortion can take various forms

Tithes and donations

While many religious communities practice tithing or donations, some leaders exploit this practice by demanding excessive amounts, promising spiritual rewards in return. Followers may be told that failing to give enough will result in divine punishment.

Promises of prosperity

Some religious figures claim they can make followers wealthy or successful if they "sow a seed" by donating a significant portion of their income or possessions. These leaders prey on vulnerable individuals who are desperate for a better life.

Selling salvation

In the most extreme cases, followers are told they must pay for salvation or access to heaven. These manipulative tactics feed on people's fear of death and the afterlife, ensuring the religious leader stays in control.

Over time, these leaders amass great wealth while their followers, driven by fear and devotion, give away everything they have.

The Power of Belief

Religious manipulation doesn't stop at money. Some leaders push their followers into acts of violence, convincing them that they are fighting a holy war. These followers are often brainwashed into believing that killing in the name of their religion will grant them a place in heaven or eternal glory. The techniques used to manipulate people into committing such horrific acts are both psychological and emotional

Promises of divine reward

Followers are told that if they die while carrying out violent acts, they will be granted an honored place in the afterlife. In some cases, this promise extends to rewards for their families, making the sacrifice seem noble.

Demonization of others

Religious extremists often paint anyone outside their belief system as enemies or sinners who deserve punishment. This "us vs. them" mentality makes it easier for followers to justify violence, as they believe they are fighting evil.

Isolation and radicalization

Many religious manipulators isolate their followers from the outside world, feeding them only the information that reinforces their views. Over time, these followers lose touch with reality and become convinced that extreme measures, even killing or self-sacrifice, are justified in the name of their faith.

In the worst scenarios, people are driven to kill others or even themselves—whether through suicide bombings or violent acts—believing they are fulfilling a divine purpose. What began as faith transforms into a dangerous weapon.

Demigods and Cult-Like Figures

In some cases, religious manipulation goes beyond traditional faith systems and takes on the form of cult-like worship of certain individuals. These self-proclaimed "demigods" often build massive followings, convincing people that they are divine beings sent to guide humanity.

These leaders often exhibit traits of narcissism and use their charisma to gain the absolute trust of their followers. They use various manipulation techniques, including

Creating dependency

Demigod-like figures make their followers completely dependent on them for spiritual and emotional support. They convince their followers that only through their guidance can they achieve salvation or happiness.

Fear and punishment

Followers are often told that disobedience will result in severe spiritual or even physical punishment. The fear of divine retribution keeps them loyal.

Emotional manipulation

These leaders play on the emotions of their followers, making them feel special or chosen. The bond created through emotional manipulation can be so strong that followers are willing to do anything for their leader.

These cult-like figures often accumulate vast wealth and power. Their followers hand over money, land, and possessions, believing that they are fulfilling a higher purpose. The leaders live in luxury, with little regard for the sacrifices their followers make.

The Corruption of Faith

While faith can inspire great good, it can also be twisted into something dangerous when it falls into the wrong hands. Manipulative religious leaders turn trust into a weapon, using fear, emotional pressure, and promises of divine reward to control their followers. They can drive people to give up their possessions, commit violence, and even sacrifice their lives—all in the name of a higher power.

The line between faith and manipulation is a fine one. For many, it's hard to distinguish genuine spirituality from the cunning tactics of a con artist. But when religion is used to exploit, extort, or justify harm, it no longer serves the greater good—it becomes a tool of deception and destruction.

As history has shown, the greatest threat isn't always the person with a weapon in hand, but the one who can manipulate others into believing they are doing something noble while committing terrible acts.

It's a reminder that faith, while powerful, must be guarded carefully, and that trust, once given, can be dangerous in the wrong hands.

Part XIII

A Visit to the Devil's Workspaces

Dark Tourism

Dark tourism is the act of visiting places that are associated with death, disaster, or tragedy. While it may sound strange at first, people are often drawn to these locations out of curiosity, a desire to understand history, or to pay respect to those who suffered. Over the years, dark tourism has grown in popularity, as travelers seek out places that tell the stories of humanity's darkest moments.

But why do people visit such places? For some, it's about learning from the past and understanding how tragedies unfolded. For others, it's a way to connect with the emotional weight of these events. Standing in a place where history changed forever can be a powerful, sometimes even healing, experience. Whether driven by curiosity, education, or reflection, dark tourism offers a chance to explore the complexities of life and death.

Let's take a look at some of the most well-known dark tourism destinations around the world

1. Auschwitz-Birkenau, Poland

Auschwitz is one of the most infamous concentration camps from World War II, where over a million people, mostly Jews, were killed during the Holocaust. Today, it stands as a museum and memorial, reminding visitors of the horrors of genocide. Walking through its gates, seeing the barracks and gas chambers, is an emotional experience. Many visit to honor the victims and to ensure that such atrocities are never forgotten.

2. Chernobyl, Ukraine

In 1986, the Chernobyl nuclear disaster shocked the world. A reactor explosion released dangerous levels of radiation, forcing the evacuation of thousands. The town of Pripyat, once bustling with life, now sits frozen in time, abandoned and eerie. Guided tours allow visitors to explore this haunting ghost town, seeing how nature has slowly reclaimed the area. For many, visiting Chernobyl is a way to witness the scale of the disaster and reflect on the dangers of nuclear energy.

3. The Catacombs of Paris, France

Beneath the streets of Paris lies a vast network of tunnels filled with the bones of over six million people. In the 18th century, overcrowded cemeteries led to the decision to move human remains into the city's underground quarries. Today, tourists can walk through these dimly lit passageways, lined with skulls and bones, learning about the city's history and its relationship with death. The Catacombs offer a chilling but fascinating look at how societies deal with mortality.

4. Ground Zero, New York City, USA

Ground Zero, the site where the Twin Towers once stood before the tragic events of September 11, 2001, is now a memorial and museum. Visitors come from all over the world to honor the nearly 3,000 lives lost in the terrorist attacks. The memorial features two reflecting pools where the towers once stood, surrounded by the names of the victims. It's a place of deep reflection, where visitors can feel the weight of the tragedy while also seeing the resilience of New Yorkers and the world.

5. Hiroshima Peace Memorial, Japan

Hiroshima is remembered as one of the two cities where atomic bombs were dropped during World War II. The Hiroshima Peace Memorial, also known as the Atomic Bomb Dome, is one of the few structures that survived the blast. The nearby museum tells the story of the bombing, its devastating aftermath, and the global impact of nuclear warfare. Visitors come to reflect on the consequences of war and to hope for peace in the future.

6. The Killing Fields, Cambodia

The Killing Fields are a series of sites where over a million people were executed by the Khmer Rouge regime during the Cambodian genocide. One of the most visited sites is Choeung Ek, where a memorial stupa filled with the skulls of victims stands as a reminder of the atrocities. The Killing Fields offer a sobering look at one of the darkest chapters in Cambodian history, where visitors can learn about the cruelty of dictatorship and the resilience of the human spirit.

7. Nanjing Massacre Memorial, China

The Nanjing Massacre Memorial Hall in China commemorates the tragic events of 1937 when Japanese troops invaded the city of Nanjing, killing an estimated 300,000 civilians. The memorial serves as a place to honor the victims and educate people about the horrors of war. Visitors walk through haunting exhibits, including graphic photos, survivor testimonies, and statues that capture the grief of the time. The museum aims to remind the world of the human cost of violence, ensuring that the memory of those who suffered is never forgotten.

Why Do People Visit These Places?

People visit these dark tourism sites for various reasons. Some are drawn by a deep curiosity about history, wanting to understand how such tragic events could happen. Others come to honor the victims, paying their respects and reflecting on the fragility of life. For many, these visits spark important conversations about human rights, justice, and how we can prevent such tragedies from repeating.

Another reason people are drawn to dark tourism is the emotional impact. These places force us to confront uncomfortable truths about human nature, war, and suffering. Being in these locations creates a strong connection to the past, giving visitors a chance to empathize with those who lived through these terrible moments.

Lastly, dark tourism reminds us of our own mortality. It makes us reflect on the fragility of life and the importance of learning from history. By visiting these places, people can gain a deeper understanding of the world and their place in it.

Dark tourism may not be for everyone, but it offers a unique and often powerful experience for those who choose to explore it. From the horrors of Auschwitz to the abandoned streets of Chernobyl, and from the tragedy of Nanjing to the devastation of Hiroshima, these places hold the stories of our shared history. They remind us of the mistakes of the past and the importance of remembering those who suffered. For many, visiting these sites is a way to honor the dead, learn from history, and reflect on the complex nature of life, death, and the choices that shape our world.

Part XIV

The Chamber of Devil's Minister

Joseph Goebbels

In the shadowy world of World War II propaganda, one man stood at the helm, crafting a toxic narrative that spread hatred and fear across Germany and much of Europe. That man was Joseph Goebbels, Adolf Hitler's Minister of Propaganda. Through manipulation, deception, and psychological tactics, Goebbels managed to turn the Nazi Party's ideology into a powerful force that swayed millions of people, making them believe in the supremacy of the Aryan race, the necessity of war, and, most devastatingly, the persecution of Jews and other minority groups.

Goebbels wasn't just a political figure; he was a master manipulator, skilled in the art of controlling information, twisting facts, and using emotions to gain the support of the masses. His work laid the groundwork for some of the darkest moments in human history, and the tactics he employed are still used by those looking to manipulate public opinion today.

Turning Ideas into a Weapon

Joseph Goebbels wasn't always a part of the Nazi movement. Born into a modest family in 1897, he initially pursued a career as a writer. However, his fiery oratory skills and keen understanding of mass psychology soon caught Hitler's attention. By 1933, Goebbels became the Minister of Propaganda, tasked with one mission to make the Nazi Party's vision the unquestionable truth in the minds of the German people.

So how did he do it? How did Goebbels manage to spread such hatred so effectively? The answer lies in his clever use of manipulation and deception tactics, along with his sharp understanding of how human psychology works.

The Big Lie

One of Goebbels' most infamous tactics was what's often called "The Big Lie." He believed that if you told a lie so colossal that no one could believe anyone would have the audacity to make it up, people would eventually accept it as truth. This tactic played out in the Nazi regime's portrayal of Jews as dangerous enemies, despite the complete lack of evidence to support such claims.

Goebbels flooded the German public with anti-Semitic propaganda, repeating lies about Jewish people controlling the economy, being responsible for Germany's problems, or plotting to destroy German culture. Through relentless repetition across radio broadcasts, newspapers, films, and public speeches, these lies started to feel like undeniable truths to a populace already struggling with economic hardship and political instability.

Playing on Fear and National Pride

Goebbels knew that humans are not always rational beings. He understood that people are more easily swayed by their emotions than by logic, and he used this to his advantage. Through propaganda, he stoked fear and a sense of victimhood in the German people. He depicted Germany as a nation surrounded by enemies, both external (like foreign powers) and internal (like Jews, communists, and others deemed "undesirable"). He painted Hitler and the Nazis as the saviors who would restore Germany to greatness.

One of his greatest psychological tricks was the creation of an "us versus them" mentality. By creating a scapegoat—the Jewish people, along with others considered inferior—Goebbels offered the German people someone to blame for their economic woes and societal troubles. When fear is high and people feel powerless, they are more likely to believe in simple solutions to complex problems. Goebbels provided just that an enemy to fight and a leader to follow.

Crafting a One-Sided Story

Goebbels understood the importance of controlling the flow of information. Early in the Nazi regime, he took control of all forms of mass communication—newspapers, radio, films, and even art. He knew that if you control what people hear, see, and read, you can control how they think.

He once famously said, "A lie told once remains a lie, but a lie told a thousand times becomes the truth." Goebbels wasn't interested in giving people access to the truth. Instead, he flooded the airwaves and papers with carefully curated, one-sided stories that supported Nazi ideology. All dissenting voices were either silenced or eliminated. By reducing people's access to alternative perspectives, Goebbels ensured that his version of reality was the only one they encountered.

This control over information created a kind of echo chamber, where the German public heard only what Goebbels wanted them to hear—over and over again—until it became their reality.

The Power of Spectacle

Goebbels also recognized the power of spectacle. He organized massive rallies, such as the famous Nuremberg rallies, where tens of thousands of people would gather to hear Hitler speak. These events were meticulously choreographed to create an overwhelming sense of unity and strength. The sea of Nazi flags, the militaristic order, and the booming speeches from Hitler were all designed to hypnotize the crowd, making them feel part of something greater than themselves.

The rallies were more than just political events; they were emotional experiences. People left feeling empowered, patriotic, and more dedicated to the Nazi cause. Goebbels used these mass gatherings to build a sense of community, turning ideology into an almost religious experience. It wasn't just about logic—it was about tapping into the deepest emotions of pride, fear, and loyalty.

Demonization

Demonization is the act of portraying someone or something as inherently evil, immoral, or wrong. It often involves distorting facts, exaggerating flaws, and painting the person as a complete villain, rather than acknowledging the complexity of their behavior or the situation. The goal of demonization is to simplify conflicts by creating a clear "bad guy," making it easier to justify extreme reactions or avoid deeper discussions. This tactic works because it plays on our emotions—fear, anger, and moral outrage. When we see someone as a villain, we stop seeing them as human. It becomes easier to dismiss their perspective, treat them unfairly, or even rally others against them.

Demonization in Politics

In politics, demonization is a common strategy used to discredit opponents, unite a group, or push through an agenda. Politicians and political parties often exaggerate the faults of their rivals, making them seem dangerous or evil to gain support from voters or distract from their own shortcomings.

Demonization in Religion

In religion, demonization is sometimes used to maintain power, enforce orthodoxy, or rally believers around a cause. Religious leaders or groups may portray outsiders, doubters, or those with differing beliefs as evil, sinful, or in league with dark forces. This creates a clear line between "us" (the righteous) and "them" (the wicked).

By demonizing outsiders or skeptics, the leader creates fear within the group. Followers are less likely to explore other viewpoints or leave the community because they've been taught to see those who question as morally corrupt or spiritually dangerous. This kind of religious demonization strengthens the leader's control, keeping followers loyal through fear and isolation.

In some cases, demonization within religious contexts can lead to extreme actions, such as shunning, exclusion, or even violence against those who are seen as "evil." It turns complex moral or spiritual questions into black-and-white battles between good and evil.

Why Do People Use Demonization?

Demonization is effective because it simplifies complex issues. It's easier to rally people against a villain than to engage in nuanced conversations or admit shared responsibility. Here's why people use demonization:

To avoid accountability: By painting someone else as the villain, people can deflect blame and avoid dealing with their own mistakes or shortcomings.

To rally support: Demonization unites people against a common "enemy," whether that's in a relationship, political campaign, or religious community.

To create moral superiority: By casting others as evil, the demonizer positions themselves (and their side) as morally righteous. This gives them the power to dictate the terms of the conflict.

To manipulate emotions: Demonization taps into strong emotions like fear, anger, and moral outrage, making people less likely to think critically or question the narrative they're being fed.

The Cost of Demonization

Demonization is a powerful manipulation tactic that turns people into villains, often oversimplifying complex issues and stoking fear and anger. Whether in personal relationships, politics, or religion, demonization creates divisions and shuts down meaningful dialogue. By turning others into "bad guys," we lose the chance to understand them, and we risk being manipulated by those who benefit from our outrage.

Turning Hatred into Action

One of the most chilling aspects of Goebbels' propaganda was his ability to dehumanize the Jewish people. Through films, posters, and articles, Jews were portrayed not just as different, but as dangerous, filthy, and subhuman. This dehumanization was a crucial step in justifying the atrocities that followed, including the Holocaust. If you can make people believe that the enemy is not fully human, it becomes much easier to rationalize violence against them.

For example, Goebbels oversaw the production of films like *"The Eternal Jew,"* which depicted Jewish people as rats or vermin. This wasn't just about creating dislike; it was about cultivating hatred so deep that violence became acceptable—necessary, even, in the eyes of the Nazi regime.

Why Did People Believe It?

The big question is Why did so many people fall for it? The answer isn't as simple as labeling the entire population as gullible or evil. The world Goebbels created was one where people were bombarded with a single narrative, day in and day out. Economic hardships, national humiliation after World War I, and a deep-seated need for a strong leader made people vulnerable to manipulation.

Goebbels gave people a simple explanation for their

problems—Germany's defeat, economic struggles, and internal conflicts were all blamed on Jews and other minorities. He gave them a vision of hope in Hitler and the Nazi Party. And when fear is high, and when people are desperate, simple answers and promises of a better future can be incredibly seductive.

By controlling information, playing on emotions, and repeating lies until they became "truth," Goebbels manipulated an entire nation into believing in a dangerous ideology.

The Legacy of Manipulation

Joseph Goebbels didn't invent propaganda, but he perfected its darkest uses. His tactics of manipulation, deception, and control created a distorted reality that fueled one of the most horrific genocides in human history. Understanding the techniques Goebbels used is essential because the same tools—fear, repetition, emotional manipulation—are still used in politics and media today.

The lesson? Always question the information you receive. Be wary of simple solutions to complex problems, and remember that those who control the narrative often control reality.

Part XV

The Unroyal Army of Mephistopheles

Deadliest Organizations in History

Throughout history, there have been organizations responsible for widespread violence and loss of life. Some were driven by ideological beliefs, others by political goals, religious fervor, or outright cruelty. Here are ten of the most deadly organizations that left dark marks on humanity.

1. Nazi Party (Germany)

Under the leadership of Adolf Hitler, the Nazi Party rose to power in Germany in the 1930s, driven by a twisted ideology of Aryan racial superiority and extreme nationalism. Their policies led to World War II and the Holocaust, the mass genocide of six million Jews, alongside millions of others, including Roma, disabled people, and political dissidents. The Nazis aimed to reshape Europe, eliminating all who didn't fit their worldview. By the war's end in 1945, they were responsible for the deaths of an estimated 50-70 million people worldwide, making them one of the deadliest organizations in human history.

2. Khmer Rouge (Cambodia)

Led by Pol Pot, the Khmer Rouge took control of Cambodia in 1975, with a vision of turning the country into a communist agrarian utopia. They evacuated cities, forcing millions into the countryside for hard labor. The regime targeted intellectuals, professionals, and anyone they deemed enemies of their brutal, extremist ideals. Over the course of just four years, the Khmer Rouge's harsh policies, forced labor, executions, and starvation resulted in the deaths of about 1.7-2 million people, nearly a quarter of Cambodia's population.

3. The Islamic State (ISIS)

Emerging from the remnants of al-Qaeda in Iraq, ISIS was founded by Abu Bakr al-Baghdadi in 2013 with the aim of establishing a global Islamic caliphate. They captured large swathes of Iraq and Syria, imposing a brutal interpretation of Islamic law. Their reign of terror included mass executions, beheadings, sexual slavery, and bombings that targeted civilians. By 2019, after losing most of their territory, they had been responsible for the deaths of an estimated 200,000 people, though their terror network and ideology persist today.

4. The Mongol Empire (Mongolia)

Led by the legendary warrior Genghis Khan, the Mongol Empire of the 13th century was one of the largest and most powerful empires in history. Genghis Khan united nomadic tribes and launched massive military campaigns across Asia and Europe. The Mongols employed brutal tactics, massacring entire cities if they resisted. Over the course of their conquests, the Mongols are believed to have killed around 40 million people, wiping out populations and civilizations in their path.

5. Al-Qaeda

Founded by Osama bin Laden in the late 1980s, Al-Qaeda gained global infamy after the 9/11 attacks in 2001, when they orchestrated the hijacking of planes that crashed into the World Trade Center and the Pentagon, killing nearly 3,000 people. Al-Qaeda's motive was to wage jihad against the West, particularly the U.S., which they viewed as enemies of Islam. Their extremist ideology inspired terror attacks worldwide, causing the deaths of tens of thousands over the years.

6. The Japanese Imperial Army (World War II)

During World War II, Japan's Imperial Army, led by Emperor Hirohito and military leaders like Hideki Tojo, committed numerous atrocities across Asia, especially in China. Their expansionist goals and desire to dominate the Pacific led to brutal campaigns like the Nanjing Massacre, where an estimated 300,000 civilians were slaughtered. Their actions across Asia led to the deaths of approximately 20 million people, both civilians and soldiers.

7. The Hutu Militias (Rwanda)

In 1994, Rwanda witnessed one of the most horrific genocides in modern history, carried out by Hutu extremist militias. Over the span of 100 days, approximately 800,000 people, mostly from the Tutsi ethnic minority, were brutally slaughtered. Driven by a long-standing ethnic rivalry, Hutu leaders spread propaganda that dehumanized the Tutsis. The militias, including the notorious Interahamwe, carried out the massacres, often using machetes and blunt weapons, with chilling efficiency.

8. The Soviet Secret Police (NKVD/KGB)

Under Joseph Stalin's rule, the Soviet secret police, first known as the NKVD and later the KGB, became instruments of state terror. Stalin's purges, especially during the Great Terror of the 1930s, targeted millions of perceived enemies of the state, including intellectuals, military officers, and ordinary citizens. Many were sent to Gulags (forced labor camps), while others were executed. Estimates suggest that Stalin's regime was responsible for the deaths of around 20 million people, either through direct executions, starvation, or imprisonment.

9. The Lord's Resistance Army (LRA)

Founded by Joseph Kony in Uganda in 1987, the Lord's Resistance Army (LRA) is a brutal rebel group that combined elements of Christianity and mysticism. Kony claimed to be a spiritual leader sent by God, but the LRA became notorious for its extreme violence, including kidnapping children to serve as soldiers and sex slaves. Over decades, the LRA's attacks in Uganda, South Sudan, and the Central African Republic killed an estimated 100,000 people and displaced millions.

10. The Ku Klux Klan (KKK)

The Ku Klux Klan, founded in the U.S. after the Civil War in 1865, is a white supremacist organization that terrorized African Americans, Jews, immigrants, and other minorities. The Klan's main motive was to maintain white dominance, often using lynching, arson, and other forms of violence to achieve their goals. At its peak, the Klan was responsible for the deaths of thousands, although exact numbers are difficult to calculate. Their hateful ideology has lingered for over a century, leading to ongoing racial violence.

11. Liberation Tigers of Tamil Eelam (LTTE)

The Liberation Tigers of Tamil Eelam (LTTE), founded by Velupillai Prabhakaran in 1976, fought for an independent Tamil state in northern Sri Lanka. They were known for pioneering suicide bombings, assassinations, and brutal guerrilla warfare during the Sri Lankan Civil War. The LTTE engaged in numerous attacks against both military and civilian targets, including the assassination of Indian Prime Minister Rajiv Gandhi. Their war with the Sri Lankan government resulted in around 80,000-100,000 deaths over nearly three decades before the group was defeated in 2009.

12. Irish Republican Army (IRA)

The Irish Republican Army (IRA) was formed to end British rule in Northern Ireland and reunite it with the Republic of Ireland. The organization split into several factions, with the Provisional IRA being the most violent during the Troubles—a violent conflict from the 1960s to 1998. Their tactics included bombings, assassinations, and guerrilla warfare against British forces and loyalist groups. The IRA's activities resulted in around 3,500 deaths, with both combatants and civilians falling victim to the violence.

13. Aum Shinrikyo (Japanese Aum Cult)

Founded by Shoko Asahara in 1984, Aum Shinrikyo was a Japanese doomsday cult that combined elements of Buddhism, Hinduism, and apocalyptic prophecy. Asahara claimed to be the reincarnation of Christ, predicting the end of the world. The cult is best known for the 1995 sarin gas attack on the Tokyo subway, which killed 13 people and injured over 1,000. The group sought to trigger a global apocalypse to usher in its vision of utopia. They killed and injured their own members as well, leading to a total death toll of several dozen.

14. People's Temple

Led by Jim Jones, the People's Temple was a cult that began as a progressive religious movement in the 1950s, promoting racial equality and social justice. However, as Jones became increasingly paranoid and authoritarian, he moved his followers to Jonestown in Guyana. In 1978, Jones orchestrated a mass murder-suicide, convincing or coercing over 900 of his followers to drink cyanide-laced punch in what is now known as the Jonestown Massacre. It remains one of the largest loss-of-life events due to a cult.

15. Heaven's Gate

Heaven's Gate was a UFO cult led by Marshall Applewhite and Bonnie Nettles, which believed that salvation could be found by ascending to a spaceship following the Hale-Bopp comet. In 1997, Applewhite convinced 39 members of the cult to commit mass suicide in order to leave their earthly bodies and board the spacecraft. The group's beliefs combined elements of Christianity, science fiction, and New Age thought, and their tragic end remains one of the most infamous cult deaths in modern history.

16. The Branch Davidians

Led by David Koresh, the Branch Davidians were an offshoot of the Seventh-Day Adventist Church. Koresh believed he was the final prophet and led a heavily armed compound near Waco, Texas. In 1993, a standoff between the Davidians and the U.S. government ended in a tragic siege. After a 51-day standoff, the compound caught fire, killing 76 people, including Koresh, women, and children. The incident is one of the deadliest in the history of cults and continues to provoke controversy regarding the role of law enforcement.

17. The Manson Family

The Manson Family, led by Charles Manson, was a cult that believed in an impending race war Manson called "Helter Skelter." In 1969, Manson convinced his followers to murder several prominent figures in Los Angeles, including actress Sharon Tate, who was eight months pregnant at the time. The Family killed nine people in a series of brutal attacks designed to incite racial tension. Manson's charisma and apocalyptic vision led his followers to commit shocking acts of violence that shook the nation.

18. The Order of the Solar Temple

The Order of the Solar Temple, led by Joseph Di Mambro and Luc Jouret, was a secretive cult that combined New Age beliefs with apocalyptic Christianity. In the 1990s, the cult believed that the end of the world was imminent and that death would lead them to a higher spiritual plane. Between 1994 and 1997, over 70 members of the cult died in mass murder-suicides across Switzerland, Canada, and France. Some were found burned, while others were shot or drugged, believing they would ascend to a better world.

19. Mossad (Israeli Intelligence Agency)

While not a cult or terrorist organization, Mossad, the Israeli intelligence agency, is known for its covert operations and targeted killings. Mossad has been involved in numerous high-profile operations, including the hunt for Nazi war criminals and the assassination of individuals considered threats to Israel. One of its most famous missions was Operation Wrath of God, where Mossad tracked down and assassinated members of the Palestinian group responsible for the 1972 Munich Olympic massacre, resulting in multiple deaths.

While Mossad operates on behalf of state security, its actions have sometimes led to the deaths of civilians, leading to controversy. These groups and organizations, despite their varied motivations, share one common thread—a legacy of death and destruction that impacted thousands, if not millions, of lives. From political uprisings to apocalyptic cults, their influence continues to serve as a reminder of the dangers posed by unchecked extremism and authoritarianism.

Part XVI

The Misunderstood Little Devil

The Childhood Trauma-a Misconception

The idea that psychopaths all have difficult childhoods marked by neglect, poverty, abuse, or emotional deprivation is a common belief, but it is an oversimplification and generalization. While some individuals with psychopathic traits may come from challenging backgrounds, not all psychopaths have such histories. Psychopathy is a complex personality disorder that involves a combination of genetic, environmental, and neurobiological factors. The notion that all psychopaths are shaped by traumatic childhoods is a fallacy, as many psychopaths come from relatively normal or even privileged upbringings.

Genetic factors

Research suggests that psychopathy has a strong genetic component, with heritability estimates ranging from 50% to 80% (Krueger et al., 2002). This means that genetic predisposition plays a significant role in the development of psychopathic traits, regardless of childhood experiences.

High-functioning psychopaths

Some individuals with psychopathic traits, often referred to as "successful psychopaths," come from affluent and well-structured families (Cleckley, 1941). These individuals may have had a relatively stable and nurturing childhood, yet still develop psychopathic traits.

Environmental factors

While adverse childhood experiences can contribute to the development of psychopathic traits, they are not the sole cause. Environmental factors such as exposure to violence, substance abuse, or social isolation can also play a role in shaping an individual's behavior (Hare, 1991).

Psychopathy spectrum

Psychopathy exists on a spectrum, with some individuals exhibiting mild, moderate, or severe traits (Hare, 2003). Not everyone with psychopathic traits will have a difficult childhood, and some may not exhibit any significant adverse childhood experiences.

Misdiagnosis

Psychopathy is often misdiagnosed or overdiagnosed, particularly in forensic settings (Blair, 2007). This can lead to the perpetuation of the stereotype that psychopaths have a difficult childhood.

People Who Rose to Fame Despite Childhood Trauma

I. Elon Musk

The entrepreneur and business magnate experienced a difficult childhood, being raised by a single mother who struggled with depression and poverty. Despite these challenges, Musk went on to become one of the most successful entrepreneurs in the world, founding companies like PayPal, SpaceX, and Tesla.

II. Nelson Mandela

The former President of South Africa experienced a difficult childhood, being raised by a traditional Thembu family and facing intense poverty and racism. Despite these challenges, Mandela went on to become one of the most influential leaders of the 20th century, leading the fight against apartheid and becoming the first black president of South Africa.

III. Steve Jobs

The co-founder of Apple experienced a difficult childhood, being adopted by a family that struggled with poverty and addiction. Despite these challenges, Jobs went on to become one of the most successful entrepreneurs in the world, revolutionizing the tech industry with innovative products like the iPhone and iPad.

IV. B.R. Ambedkar

The Indian social reformer and lawyer experienced a difficult childhood, being born into a lower caste and facing intense social and economic oppression. Despite these challenges, Ambedkar went on to become one of the most influential figures in Indian history, leading the fight for social justice and equality.

V. Malala Yousafzai

The Nobel Peace Prize laureate experienced a difficult childhood, being raised in a region of Pakistan where girls were denied access to education. Despite these challenges, Yousafzai went on to become one of the most influential voices for girls' education, advocating for the rights of girls and women around the world.

VI. J.K. Rowling

The author of the Harry Potter series experienced a difficult childhood, being raised by a single mother who struggled with depression and poverty. Despite these challenges, Rowling went on to become one of the most successful authors of all time.

VII. Stephen King

The horror writer experienced a troubled childhood, being raised in a family that struggled with poverty and addiction. King has spoken publicly about the impact of his childhood on his writing, but he has also gone on to become one of the most successful authors in the world.

VIII. Oprah Winfrey

The media mogul experienced childhood trauma, being molested by a family member and struggling with poverty. Despite these challenges, Winfrey went on to become one of the most influential women in the world, building a media empire and inspiring millions of people.

VIX. Richard Branson

The entrepreneur and founder of Virgin Group experienced a difficult childhood, being dyslexic and struggling in school. Despite these challenges, Branson went on to build a business empire and become one of the most successful entrepreneurs in the world.

X. Ratan Tata

The iconic Indian industrialist, is a story of resilience and vision. Born into the famous Tata family, Ratan faced a turbulent childhood due to his parents' separation when he was just 10 years old. Raised by his grandmother, Lady Navajbai Tata, he endured emotional struggles that shaped his character early on. Despite these challenges, he went on to study at Cornell and Harvard, later joining Tata Steel as a worker on the shop floor to understand the industry from the ground up. His rise to fame came when he took over as Chairman of the Tata

Group in 1991, transforming the conglomerate into a global powerhouse. Under his leadership, Tata Motors launched the revolutionary Tata Nano, and Tata acquired international brands like Jaguar Land Rover and Tetley Tea. Ratan Tata's journey is a testament to overcoming personal hardships and leading with integrity and innovation.

The Importance of Resilience

These examples highlight the importance of resilience in overcoming childhood trauma. While it's true that some people who experience childhood trauma may be more likely to develop psychopathic traits, it's not a universal truth. In fact, many people who experience childhood trauma go on to lead successful and fulfilling lives.

The Role of Environment and Support

The environment and support system can play a significant role in determining whether someone who experiences childhood trauma will develop psychopathic traits. For example, someone who has a supportive family and access to resources may be less likely to develop psychopathic traits, even if they experience childhood trauma.

For example, someone who has a supportive family and access to resources may be less likely to develop psychopathic traits, even if they experience childhood trauma.

In conclusion, the notion that psychopaths have a difficult childhood marked by neglect, poverty, cruelty from parents, sexual or other abuse, or emotional deprivation is a generalization that doesn't hold up to scrutiny. While it's true that some people who experience childhood trauma may be more likely to develop psychopathic traits, it's not a universal truth. In fact, many people who experience childhood trauma go on to lead successful and fulfilling lives, demonstrating the importance of resilience and the role of environment and support in determining outcomes.

Bibliography

1. Influence: The Psychology of Persuasion by Robert B. Cialdini

2. The 48 Laws of Power by Robert Greene

3. The Psychopath Test: A Journey Through the Madness Industry by Jon Ronson

4. Dark Psychology: Super Advanced Techniques to Persuade Anyone" by John Clark

5. The Sociopath Next Door: The Ruthless Versus the Rest of Us by Martha Stout

6. The Anatomy of Human Destructiveness by Erich Fromm

7. Without Conscience: The Disturbing World of the Psychopaths Among Us by Robert D. Hare

8. The Confidence Game: Why We Fall for It... Every Time by Maria Konnikova

9. Cultish: The Language of Fanaticism by Amanda Montell

10. The Lucifer Effect: Understanding How Good People Turn Evil by Philip Zimbardo

11. The Dark Psychology of Manipulation: The Complete Guide to Persuasion and Manipulation by William Cooper

12. People of the Lie: The Hope for Healing Human Evil by M. Scott Peck

13. Toxic People: 10 Ways of Dealing with People Who Make Your Life Miserable" by Lillian Glass

Websites:

1. Psychology Today

https://www.psychologytoday.com

2. The Crime Report

https://thecrimereport.org

3. Robert Hare's Psychopathy Research

http://www.hare.org

4. Manipulative-People.com

https://manipulative-people.com

5. Mind Hacks

https://mindhacks.com

6. Verywell Mind

https://www.verywellmind.com

7. The Conversation - Psychology Section

https://theconversation.com/us/psychology

8. Scientific American: Mind

https://www.scientificamerican.com/mind/

9. A&E's Crime and Investigation Blog

https://www.aetv.com

10. Simply Psychology

https://www.simplypsychology.org

11. Medium's Psychology Section

https://medium.com/tag/psychology

12. Dark Psychology and Manipulation

https://darkpsychology.co

13. Quackwatch

https://www.quackwatch.org

14. All About Psychology

https://www.all-about-psychology.com

15. Academia.edu

https://www.academia.edu

16. Forbes - Leadership and Manipulation

https://www.forbes.com

17. Crimereads

https://crimereads.com

18. The Skeptic's Dictionary

http://www.skepdic.com

19. Narcissist Abuse Support

https://narcissistabusesupport.com

20. Conman.com

https://conman.com

ABOUT THE AUTHOR

Dr. Robin K. Mathew is an accomplished psychologist and ethnographer with a deep understanding of human behavior, gained through extensive, global experience. As a social psychology analyst, he has contributed to various media platforms, drawing from his diverse professional background and his interactions with individuals from nearly 90 different nationalities. His career, rich with cross-cultural engagement, reflects a deep appreciation of the complex socio-economic, ethnic, and linguistic differences that shape human experience.

With formal education and professional experience in fields such as information technology, human resource management, psychology, cyber forensics, and cyber psychology, Dr. Mathew has worked with esteemed institutions including the University of Toronto, Best Buy, the Indian Institute of Management, ICFAI Business School, the Royal Bank of Canada, and Michigan University. These roles have provided him with an unparalleled ability to connect the dots between various disciplines, enriching his psychological insight.

Over the past twelve years, Dr. Mathew has authored nearly 500 articles across a wide range of subjects, published in prestigious magazines both in India and internationally. His writing captures the intricate nuances of human nature, informed by the vast knowledge he has accumulated throughout his career. In addition to his articles, he has successfully authored and published 15 books, each delving deeply into different facets of psychology, offering readers a profound exploration of the human condition.

Through this journey, Dr. Mathew has cultivated not just expertise, but also a uniquely global perspective—an asset he brings to every project, publication, and platform he works with

Other books by the Author:
Malayalam

1. Madamballiyille Manorogikal
2. Chekuthante Panipura
3. Chanakyante Kamukimar
4. Digital Nagavallimar
5. Cyber Parakaya Pravesham
6. Oru Kanyakayude Suvishesham
7. Jeevitha Vijyathinte Krithrima Thakkol
8. Kaanan Desham Thedi Poyavar

English

1. Lovers of Chanakya
2. In Quest of the Promised Land
3. I am Akira
4. The Expedition of Nun
5. The Artificial Key to Success
6. The Psychology of Mind Deception
7. Human Algorithm-Cyber Psychology for the Digital Age

Email: robinkmathew@gmail.com

www.ingramcontent.com/pod-product-compliance
Lightning Source LLC
LaVergne TN
LVHW091149150826
845672LV00005B/1081

* 9 7 8 9 3 6 0 8 3 8 5 0 8 *